Godfrey

from

Ronald

Nov. 1983.

D1492185

# DIARY OF A COLONIAL
# OFFICER'S WIFE

# DIARY OF
# A COLONIAL OFFICER'S
# WIFE

*by*

*Laura Boyle*

**COLLINS**
St. James's Place London
1970

ISBN 0 00 211165 9

© this edition Laura Boyle 1970
originally published 1968 by Alden Press

TYPESET BY MONOPHOTO IN 11 PT. BASKERVILLE
PRINTED OFFSET BY ALDEN & MOWBRAY LTD, OXFORD
BOUND AT THE KEMP HALL BINDERY

# PREFACE

My wife's decision to try and publish her 1916/17 diary when with me in Ashanti and the Gold Coast was entirely due to a letter she had read in the 'Times' during 1965. This had been written by Dame M. Perham to former members of the Colonial Service informing them of the establishment of a Record Office in Oxford which will contain, not only papers formerly housed at the Colonial Office in London (at its end), but also for the reception of diaries, personal letters and historial commentaries which are still extant in private ownership.

These papers will if sorted create a national picture of when, how and where, framing the traditional background of the duties, the growth of an unique spirit of racial influence which will be a model peep into the past, and above all, they will be invaluable to students and others who are without personal knowledge of the real leadership and training within the Empire in many countries in the world.

After thinking it out with me as to how best to make a start and see whether some apparent interest might be created at any rate in one article, before tackling the problem of a book as a whole, we decided to try the 'Woman's Journal', and shortened the first chapter to an article and one or two illustrations. Only a few days elapsed before a delightful letter from the Editor of the 'Woman's Journal' offered to buy forthwith the first rights of publication on the article, with permission to use it if publishing a book at a later date. This we thought might help to create interest, and the deal was done then and there.

Others must also be thanked, and my wife's warmest appreciation of their help and advice must go to Sir Charles Ponsonby who suggested my trying the Alden Press at Oxford as he himself did for his own much better life story, Miss Juliet O'Hea for advice and suggestions and last but not least, Sir Compton Mackenzie who has known the author for many years and, in spite of his amazingly busy life has written of the value he thinks this book may be in these critical times.

*David Boyle*

# FOREWORD

"How fortunate I have been! To get engaged at home during the first years of our 1914 war, and now married and accompanying my husband back to his District in West Africa where I was to find myself embarking on a life of official administration with the chance of learning to know and appreciate the Ashanti people, the Hausa, and other races."

And how fortunate David Boyle was to have a wife able to keep a diary so vivid that the fifty years which have rolled by since then roll away and make this diary so perfect an evocation of the past.

At this moment when racial relations are such a problem I cannot refrain from expressing my gratitude for the way the contemporary evidence of Laura Boyle's Diary demonstrates what a remarkably efficient and conscientious body the representatives of British colonialism were. I wish that a few of the more intelligent young people of today could read this evidence. The uninformed and immature attitude to an imaginary blimpish tyranny in West Africa is matched by the equally uninformed and immature attitude towards the old Indian Army.

I was fortunate enough twenty years ago to be given an opportunity to appreciate the achievement of that Indian Army when at its peak that Indian Army ceased to exist. I was never fortunate enough to visit the Gold Coast or Ashanti in the days when colonialism was still making West Africa a peaceful part of the world. Yet by reading this Diary I find I can appreciate the achievement of those District Officers of once upon a time.

I am grateful for this opportunity to salute them.

*Compton Mackenzie*

# CONTENTS

# ILLUSTRATIONS

# CONTENTS

# ILLUSTRATIONS

# CHAPTER I

# Coomassie to Wenchi

August 5th, 1916: Coomassie.

It was late in the evening that our train after its eleven hours journey from the Gold Coast emerged from the dense forest country and landed us in the capital of Ashanti. Tired as we were by the jerking movement of our saloon carriage as the train climbed its way past the gold mining country in the pressing heat of the day, there was a thrill of historical pleasure when the Acting Chief Commissioner (Mr. Philbrick) conducted David and myself across the wide open maidan to the old Fort which had become so well known to the outer world in the 1900 siege.

How fortunate I had been! To get engaged at home during the first years of our 1914 war, and now married and accompanying my husband back to his District in West Africa where I was to find myself embarking on a life of official administration, with the chance of learning to know and appreciate the Ashanti people, the Hausas, and other races.

Few women in these days of war had the chance of really living among the many tribes of West Africa, and of learning enough of the languages to have the added pleasure of helping in the fatherly rule that the Colonial Service rendered from the Gambia to Nigeria. Along the coast most of the towns had a fair complement of European wives but the hinterland saw little of them. North of the Coomassie area many of the Districts had never had a white woman as a permanent resident, and I was inwardly very proud, though perhaps slightly nervous, that I would be living in one which had not been so favoured since the Ashanti war.

Although we had landed at Seccondee from the mail boat only three days ago, I soon felt quite at home as regards the native element since my husband's police orderly (Moussa), his two boys (house and cook), and a small girl to be my personal maid, had met us on arrival and were already doing our domestic tasks and anticipating our wishes as if they had served us for years. It all seemed quite natural.

Followed by them, and a squad of carriers, we entered by the main gate of the Fort with its smart W.A.F.F. sentries, and were soon up the stairs that led to the Chief Commissioner's own house and looking out over the wide expanse of open ground between us and the town as a whole. Out of sight the regimental band of the garrison was playing its weekly programme in front of the Officers Mess, while an occasional sound of drums or other music drifted to us on the other side. An early bed, well fortified by large mosquito nets, succeeded the evening meal, and we both slept like tired sheepdogs until awakened on the Sunday morning by Mama and Tani bearing the early morning tea and fruit, and anxious to know our orders as to baths, clothes and general requirements. As we will be going on North in two or three days, it was not easy to extract things necessary at once.

This 6th August being Sunday, we were lucky to have struck a first day which had no official coming and going in the office, and so were glad of the rest that Sunday called for even in the African world. Our host didn't appear until lunch time, before which we did a little walk outside the Fort and a small private service by ourselves in the drawingroom. In the early afternoon we loitered in the garden as well as making our way down to the well which in the 1900 siege was the only place from which water could be got (there was *none* in the Fort then), and to which the surrounding Ashanti chiefs and armies allowed the English Garrison half an hour twice a day to get water. They explained this by saying that they could not fight others who were unable to get water for themselves.

It rained quite hard as darkness fell, and while we had dinner to which the P.M.O. and the P.W.D. Senior Officers came, the noise at times drummed loudly on the verandah outside the large dining-room overlooking the maidan. Before dinner I had one or two awkward moments as Tani (only about 13 years old) couldn't understand why I wanted to bath by myself, and had insisted on accompanying me with towels and all that; she only talks Hausa so we cannot yet converse at all, and all I could do was to plunge hurriedly into the bath, scrub myself like lightning, leap out and grab the big bath towel she was holding for me, and then let her do something ordinary like brushing my hair! It really was quite funny.

Monday August 7th dawned fine and cool (the rainy days in the Ashanti forest belt are apparently always hot and uncomfortable), and we joined Mr. Philbrick at breakfast after which I tried the piano in the drawing-room while David went off with Moussa to the railway station to check up on our loads for the North.

He was kept pretty busy by this all day, so that everything we had brought out with us could be accounted for, and then allocated by weight to the carriers who are to accompany us to Wenchi; a large number of the boxes contain food supplies of all kinds, provided in those days for many Colonial officers by Fortnum & Mason, and ranging from soap and candles to tinned peaches, butter, sausages and so on – in fact enough to stock a District Officer's house for at least nine or ten months; fresh food and vegetables depended on the local villages and cultivation.

The rest of that day, and the following one, were spent in buying a few things in the town, visiting the Bank and the Post Office, meeting various officials, and to our boys delight, purchasing two second-hand bicycles for them which will enable them to get ahead of the carriers when we tour in the district from village to village.

August 10th dawned gray and misty which augured well for my first journey into the 'bush', and after a cheerful early breakfast and having finally completed our personal packing, I looked over the verandah at the amazing scene in the court-yard below where our carriers (they are government employed) were assembling each behind the load allocated to him, with David in khaki uniform accompanied by a clerk who checked the men as they adjusted the pads on their heads and lined up in rows. All this satisfactorily arranged, the long procession filed out of the Fort's main gate accompanied by a policeman and the two youngest servants, Tani with a large enamel basin filled with plates on her head and carrying a lantern, with the small boy in a dirty cotton overall and Homburg hat leading a monkey on a string! It was an amusing sight at the start of a 95 miles odd journey to our District H.Q. which is called Wenchi.

For the rest of the morning David and I remained quietly in the Fort until luncheon which Philbrick (his usual morning's office work done) had with us, so as to be able to say farewell to us immediately the meal was over. Sharman, the P.W.D. chief, had arranged for his car to take us up the first 5½ miles to the junction of the Northern Territories road and the Kimtampo one which is ours. There the hammock boys would be waiting for us to climb into our hammocks.

Before we could start however one of the hammock men reported that he had met a man on the road who had stolen a load from him two years ago, so that had to be enquired into on the spot; the enquiry ended by the man being arrested and taken along with us. This began our real trek to Wenchi, my hammock going first on the heads of four boys with two in reserve to change places from time to time and carrying such things as a chair, a sunshade, my shooting stick and other knick-knacks. Moussa, looking very smart in uniform, followed me, and behind him came David with his 6 boys (2 in reserve). It was forest all the way with small farms by the road, cocoa, bananas, and root crops, about six small villages, and crossing little streams from time to time, we had started in our hammocks about 3.15 p.m. and arrived at Kwaman (7-8 miles) at 5.15; but I got there well ahead of David who had been delayed by the prisoner running off into the bush, and then when caught falling flat on the road and pretending he was dead!

The Kwaman rest-house is a low one-storey bungalow with a little verandah and arrangement of windows and doors all open and no glass, so that the flying insects, ants, sandflies and other horrid creatures have their own way as I soon began to realize! Outside there was a small open patch with some Barbadoes pride, and in the compound some huts for the boys. Ours had been there well ahead of us, and had set out our beds, baths, chairs and boxes which supplemented the scanty rest-house furniture of 2 tables and 4 or 5 chairs. The village chief came up with his linguist, and David spoke to him for a few minutes, thanking him for the 'dash' he had brought consisting of 4 chickens, 8 eggs and a yam; being a small and poor village this was quite a decent offering. ('Dash' is the term used everywhere in these Districts for the present of food all heads of villages, or tribal Kings, make to a Commissioner on his arrival; they are publicly thanked for, and privately re-imbursed in a gift of cash by the officer's clerk on leaving). The prisoner was then put into the Chief's charge to be sent next day to Coomassie for trial, and after we had eaten Ali's excellent dinner of tomato soup, roast chicken, yam, Indian corn, and lime juice we turned in quite ready for bed after what to me was an unusual and exciting day.

Friday August 11th saw us rising at 5.30 a.m. dressing by lantern light, having breakfast ditto, and starting out in the grey mist at 6.15 to walk as long as we could in the cool hours of the day. I managed 3 hours at quite a good pace, and then took to the hammock, D. following my example in that way about an hour later; Mama and Ali stayed behind to make sure of all the carriers and their loads starting together, and then with their bicycles passed us all to organize preparations at the village where we proposed to take luncheon. Moussa on these journeys always remains with his master, but we had another policeman Ahmedu with us this trip, who was going to be in charge of the Wenchi prison so both ourselves and the carriers were well watched over.

All was thick forest as before until we came to the river Offin which was more like one than the usual little streams across the road; it was in fact when south of Coomassie the boundary between the Gold Coast and Ashanti. The carriers got us both across that by making four-handed seats, and everyone else waded through without mishap. What interested me there was the extraordinary number and beauty of the butterflies, some quite enormous, of all colours, blue, orange, green, red, black or white which seemed to gather particularly around forest openings where there is water and air to bask or flutter happily in. Against the dull green of the giant forest trees the colours stood out in increased refulgence; I was already rather tired of the sameness of the Ashanti 'bush' so welcomed the butterfly distraction. Today we managed to travel some 18 miles, and ended up at a village called Chichiwere which David said was the dirtiest and most uncared-for one he had ever come across –

not even the road was kept properly open, a task which in all Districts is that of a village or town for a certain distance each way. Added to this bit of bad work, our carriers were so late arriving that they had to be told off in no uncertain terms; it was well on in the evening before peace and satisfaction returned to all of us, and then at last we slept all out and nothing mattered.

Next day was one quite unlike the usual 12th August in Scotland and its thoughts of grouse on the moors! Here in Africa we dressed hurriedly by yellow candlelight, and having eaten our breakfast in half daylight started soon after 6.0 to find that the forest was far more open, and the road led gradually into wider spaces of country but still without much of a view in any direction. After 3 hours or so we came to a whacking big hill and a rain-washed track between huge boulders and red rocks. We got out of our hammocks and scrambled up until more undulating ground enabled us to ride in the hammocks again, and then reached a small village called Eyemasu where the road was once more in splendid order—a broad red track with pleasant green trees and bushes on each side, full of sunlight. We stopped at one end of it, and sat on camp chairs in the middle of the road to drink some welcome tea from our Thermos flasks, and talk with the Chief congratulating him on his road work. At the other end the women of the village were all out cleaning the road, many with their babies on their backs or beside them. We then passed through a pleasant little bit of orchard country, open with tall grass and scattered small trees, until a sudden stretch of really remarkably good wide and level road inspired our hammock boys to jog smoothly along at about 6 miles an hour all the way to Secheredumasi where a great crowd of people came tumbling out of the village with drums and trumpets which they rolled and blew to welcome us.

Here we were swept up to the rest-house in great style led by a man with a stick of office and a great Union Jack, then David in his hammock and I in mine—our own various followers trailing out behind. The Chief ran with the best of them, a blue silk scarf round his neck coming undone in the process—little boys running beside us clutching their own toga-like garment, until all halted at the rest-house door where David stepped out and thanked them for our reception, and we disappeared inside to rest and await Ali's good luncheon which he was then

6

preparing.

After devouring an egg and onion omelette, cold chicken, tinned cherries, and salted ground nuts which are as seductive as burnt almonds, we spent the afternoon in long chairs, with some 'shut eye', some books, and pen and ink, until we felt strong enough to face the locals again. By this time the Chief and a select party of his principal villagers had gathered outside, the Chief himself sitting in the middle of them on his 'stool' which is the moveable throne all the Ashanti Chiefs and kings have and are carried about with them when on official occasions. The actual 'stool' is a low wooden chair studded with brass nails or if a great chief with golden ones, the principal servant holding a large decorative umbrella over his master's head when sitting, and carries it alongisde him when moving about. The rest sat around him, silent and immoveable like grave brown statues with the inevitable printed cotton cloth thrown over one shoulder; lots of little boys were also present on the outskirts of the official group out to see what the 'bature' (big man or boss) had to say. Moussa put two chairs out for us in front of the delegation, and we stalked out backed by our two police orderlies. David then spoke to the assembled crowd while a roadman (a native of those parts) interpreted very well; this David could check as he had already passed his exam in Twi, the Ashanti language, but could not entirely rely on his knowledge. Anyhow it was the custom to speak through a linguist, a very good idea too as both sides can hear what is said before having to reply! He complimented them all on the good road, and the clean village, told them a bit about the war and how it was progressing, informed them that Fuller (the Chief Commissioner) was back from leave and had gone to see the Governor (Sir Hugh Clifford) at Accra before coming to see them, and sent them away completely happy. Not being David's own district, the Chief and his people would not ask him for any necessities or make complaints; for that, they had to deal with their own District Officer who visited them regularly.

A little later we inspected the village, and particularly the work on the new main road with gutters and well drained. On one side of it there were a few Hausas from the North in their white caps and gallabeyahs who were selling meat as they

7

apparently do when travelling south to the forest country. This village was very disloyal sixteen years ago, but now are firm supporters of our rule and the opening up of trade by new roads. Round the rest-house, and indeed round the village as a whole, there was quite a bit of open country with birds of many kinds flying to and fro: this especially interested me as we had seen (except for a few wicked looking vultures) hardly any since leaving the Fort. Here there were hornbills, green pigeons, and others, some looking for fruit among the lime trees, and many more flying to the bigger trees on the forest fringe. We sat in front of the rest-house overlooking all this, and brightened by zinnias and Barbadoes pride; hornets seemed active, but avoided us thank goodness.

The following day, a Sunday, we did our usual early break-fast and departure, stepping out briskly in a grey cool morn through open grass and tree, flat, country, and actually com-pleted some 24 miles, our best journey since leaving Coomassie. On the road we met many Hausas and Fulanis—drovers—who were driving cattle and sheep from the North like the few we saw yesterday. To my unaccustomed eyes it seemed odd to be engaged in such a peaceful profession when carrying swords or huge knives or bright spears. One of the men had a black cotton umbrella with silver beads on it in one hand, three spears in the other, and a large knife slung over his shoulder in a leather sheath!

We next hammocked on to the Pru river which fortunately was very low: after the crossing came a small village about 11.30 where we decided to rest both ourselves and the carriers, and take an early luncheon, being more than half-way on our proposed long trek, and the carriers could get a second wind before they got too weary. It was a pleasant spot, on one side palm-thatched yellow mud houses with groups of people, behind us an open air butcher's shop, a large baobab tree shading us from the now well-risen sun, and after a quarter of an hour or so, two tables with a good meal set before us. Ali is really a marvel: they do wonders in this country with an open fire on the ground with the aid of a cook-box.

At 12.30 the march was resumed with the hammock boys going like birds, hot as it now was. They had nearly all been in the Cameroons with the troops, and one of D.'s men (quite a wit) had picked up a lot of English expressions such as: 'Sergeant Major I want to see them prisoner'—or 'Black man, no fear' while the others during their run shouted out their own extraordinary words. For instance one would say 'Sibbe'—another 'Suba'—'Sokli'—'Daouny'—'Mo! Mo! Mo!' and so on. I certainly enjoyed all this, but even in the hammock I began to sweat furiously, and like the boys was glad when we reached N'koranza, our first really important tribal town. Out came the familiar mob of people and drums and noise amid which we very quickly reached the rest-house. There from the verandah David thanked the Omanhin, or King, for our reception, and we both shook hands with him. He is quite a young man, and looked very shy; he had two enormous gold rings on, one with spikes sticking out of it! Later the 'dashes' arrived, yams, chickens, eggs and a sheep; this latter will be given to the carriers tomorrow. We had tea on the verandah; it is clear all round, and in front is a broad red earth road leading to the village which is just out of sight.

N'koranza was known to be a very disloyal centre in 1900, but thanks to the Queen Mother (who is still alive) it managed to get through and remain loyal in spite of some of its younger sub-chiefs. The present young king is kept severely under her thumb together with a group of older men who were with him today. The Ashanti are all matriarchally ruled, and though the Chief may be married, it is not necessarily his son who suceeds—that is settled by *his* mother who behind the scenes has all powers over the family. Being one of the five greatest tribes in Ashanti, the Omanhin is entitled to a Union Jack and to a large silver-topped staff called 'a message stick'. David has one with him, and it was sent on to the next village (Tekiman) where we are due tomorrow so that preparations could be made there: it is the first one in David's own District, and the King is the most important of all his chiefs.

In the early evening came wonderful news: the mail had arrived! The first news from home since we left on July 18th, so was especially welcome, and we spent the whole evening reading letters from our relations and friends, and learning with jealousy how those at Fairlie were bathing in glorious weather which began after we left. It made me smell and taste the salt tang, hear the gulls crying, and feel the sweet west wind from the

the hills of Arran: but Providence aye knows what's best for us, and this is all very exciting and adventurous anyhow.

Next day, August 14th, was a horrid, long, and weary one although it seems rather amusing now it's over, nearly 10 hours of travelling including $1\frac{1}{2}$ hours for luncheon and $1\frac{1}{2}$ for being lost in the bush! We soon left the good road, which went due North to Kintampo, and after a village called Dumasi some 3 miles from our start took a cleared bush road thinking it had been cleared by the people knowing of our coming. This actually led us past some yam and ground nut farms, eventually ending abruptly. Then we tried another path through elephant grass, palms and forest gradually crowding in on us: Moussa, David and I (on foot, all of us) in front—then some carriers and hammockmen, slashing and cutting when unable to get through —but that also become hopeless. I got very hot and fractious, so after a little more unrewarded wandering we threw our hands in and struggled back to the village. As we were entering it, one of the carriers unearthed an elderly Ashanti woman from the long grass who, when asked why the path that led nowhere had been cleaned up, cackled with laughter, and said it was done because a cocoa farm was going to be established there!

We, thank goodness, got back to the place where the big road had broken off from our required path, and by following the telegraph wires discovered a rotten little track on which we could see the bicycle marks, so we knew that Mama and Ali had gone that way. Our original idea of arriving at Tekiman in time for a late luncheon was now a physical impossibility, so rather disgruntled we took to our hammocks and were carried along without much alacrity as everyone was fairly tired already; the track was bad and mostly up and down—as a result of which one of my leading boys fell suddenly, throwing me out and hurting his leg in the process. David got out of his hammock at once, and others rushing up to help, we straightened things out—the team was reconstituted, and although angry words flew for a bit we got moving again. The injured lad was left by himself on the road, which I though rather cruel, but 'no'; he hirpled into the next village where we luckily found luncheon and our boys awaiting us, and it was obvious that his fellows knew he wasn't bad, and only needed a rest, or they would not have gone on without him.

Our luncheon was indeed a surprise, as Mama and Ali had naturally gone on towards Tekiman but finding that we had not arrived at Forikum (the village we had now reached), they had stayed there and had everything ready, chairs, table, food and all, in the village street. Everyone was glad of the un-expected stop, but there was not too much time to spare as we pushed off again as rain fell—yet another bit of bad luck on this day of misfortunes. The track was soon the usual overgrown apology for a path, and had all kinds of surprises, a period of large rocks surrounded by long grass and small trees—then more orchard country—then a bit of deep forest—hot, steamy, uneven ground, and although I had walked some of it to be like the others, it was no good and I had to get back into my hammock and long for the end of our tribulations.

At last, three hours or more later than we had planned, we reached a freshly cleaned bit of track, improving thereafter every hundred yards. Before long we fell in with a crowd of children and young people, supported by a nice cheery-faced elderly black man dressed in a sort of blue serge (the Head of the Wesleyan School here)—who gave us a welcome and pro-ceeded to sing what sounded like a mixture of hymns, rhymes and ballads. This stirred the hammock boys who began to break into a run. Next we met the Chief of Tekiman and his suite, who preceded us to the rest-house. We are now in David's own District, and the rest-house was built under his supervision last year. It has two main rooms inside, and a wide verandah all round with a deep thatched grass roof with eaves which makes it continually cool; there are no ceilings—the roof covers it all. Everything was soon arranged by the boys and the sheep 'dashed' yesterday was given to the wounded carrier for him and his fellows to eat tomorrow when we will be staying here the whole day. The compound in which the rest-house is built contains a kitchen, servants' huts, and other rooms for spare kit. After tea we slacked and bathed, had dinner, played patience and finally, after the most fatiguing day of my life having been lost in the bush, thrown out of my hammock, marched for 4 hours under the actinic rays of a tropical sun, I feel I have some excuse for lightness in my head so 'I will put this writing book away, with nobody to say me nay'.

August 15th began badly as still rather bemused by yesterday's events I got out of the wrong side of my bed at 7.10 a.m., but a well-timed homily from my good man restored me to a right frame of mind! Tani then brushed my hair with ever increasing skill and a first class leisurely breakfast with three tiny fresh eggs equipped me for what became a most interesting day. The 'dashes' here were not only from Tekiman himself, but also from the Head of the Hausa Zongo and from a Moshi headman as well—they consisted of 2 sheep, about 50 eggs, 3 fowls, and 10 yams—next day at Wenchi both our servants and the police will receive one of the sheep which means general rejoicing. We are now on the main Wenchi-Coomassie road, having come the other way as shorter—and for testing the new bit of the Kintampo road on our way. After breakfast, accompanied by the two orderlies we walked down to the Zongo with its mixture of Northern races, and its small market, but only spent a short time as we expected the Omanhin's official call during the morning. And so it was, for we had hardly returned to the rest-house before the cacophony of drums and music made it known that the King was on his way.

The procession quite took my breath away. A packed crowd came up the hill with two men carrying enormous state umbrellas, others several stools (or thrones), others things that looked like sceptres but were really swords, and other insignia. This marvellous assemblage grouped themselves down opposite our front door like a well-arranged photograph, and indeed when David moved out to greet them he asked permission to take a photograph before entering on the official proceedings. The Omanhin was quite upset because he hadn't his best clothes on, but he looked smart enough to my mind. This Mephistophelian looking gentleman sat on his best stool (gold knobs and nails) and preened himself for the operation! Taking his crown, a black leather helmet like a German pickelhaube only with a gold rim to it and studded with lumps of rough gold, from the man whose duty it was to carry it, he placed it firmly on his head. His dress consisted of a voluminous toga-like Jacob's coat of many colours (actually known as a Kettah cloth, and only worn by the great) entirely made up of small square patches of every colour under the sun. On his feet were leather sandals, round his neck two or three leather necklaces, and his hands and arms were simply laden with gigantic gold bracelets and rings of extraordinary patterns in the shapes of scorpions, tortoises, suns with spiky rays sticking out of them and so on., All this was completed by a purple and gold silk handkershief carried in a negligée fashion in one gilded hand. After the photograph was taken he took his crown off and put several things on his head that looked like necklaces made of pieces of gold and leopard skin, and I don't know what! I thought he looked very like my idea of a young Nero with his funny rather sulky face, drooping eyelids, and extraordinary diagonal wrinkles on his forehead. The Wesleyan schoolmaster in his blue serge suit who was to interpret made a quaint contrast to this barbaric splendour.

The palaver now began. I sat just inside the doorway, and David on a chair outside where he made a speech. This was interpreted by the schoolmaster to the King's linguist who stood beside his lord and said 'Uh-Ha' just like any good Lowland Scot, and 'Yo' or 'Oh Yeh' after every few words. It was as good as a play and as funny as a barrel of monkeys. After David ended his address, the Omanhin arose and began a long harangue with much perturbation of be-ringed hands, stroking his chin, rolling his eyes, beating the air, pointing heavenwards, and generally behaving like Punch and Judy. This in its turn was interpreted to David. There was a long yarn about the 'young man's party'* which were trying to 'de-stool' him, and then how necessary it was for David to help him—and other district matters which had to be gone into by the Government. Some more backchat of a satisfactory nature from David and the business came to an end, with all smiling happily.

Now I stepped into the limelight and shook hands with the Chief who at D.'s request showed me all his jewellery which made him as pleased as a child. He saw my engagement ring (they never use precious stones, only gold) which fascinated him so much that he promptly offered one or two of his own in exchange, and my gold wrist watch amused him greatly so that he laughed and jabbered like a baby with a new toy. Then the procession moved off to the same riotous accompaniment of drums and music while we were left in peace to have our luncheon, a special treat since for the first time I was to sample 'groundnut', the great African dish, as a rule only indulged in on Sundays because it is so filling that no one can ever do more work after it, so the afternoon is entirely a long rest. This fearsome dish is compounded of groundnut soup, bits of chicken, whole eggs, rice, fu-fu (a paste of pounded-up yams or bananas), peppers, and okros, a very good green native vegetable. After partaking of this vast feed which is really 3 or 4 courses in one, we tackled a few tinned strawberries, and mutually agreed that bed or a long chair was essential; at least an hour or more of the afternoon passed in this way. When the Africans themselves feast on groundnut, they swell up prodigiously but luckily our tummies don't behave in that puppy-like fashion!

There was rain in the afternoon, and when it stopped we decided that the official duties had all been dealt with, and that a private stroll round the village and its outskirts would be nice in the cool of the evening. Accompanied by Moussa carrying my sunshade we took the broad red road which was glowing in the light of the evening sun and toured some of the shops—Millers, for example, (the kind of 'Army & Navy' of the Gold Coast and most other West Coast towns), the Zongos, the Wesleyan School and to my great pleasure discovered the source of the water supply, a clear bubbling stream coming out of the forest only a few yards above the road; very different this from the sluggish muddy waters seen in the central forest zone further South. At the school there were children of all ages: 16, 15, 14 down to little ones of 5 and under. Two of the older ones read bits out of 'Jack of the Beanstalk'. The little ones voiced the Alphabet, and one boy asked by David as to what he wanted to be when grown up said firmly 'a man of God' i.e. a missionary.

When we left to a singing of a hymn, and a final 'God Save the King', we felt it was quite a good show, and hastened to return to the rest-house for dinner and so to bed.

August 16th. The final day's trek to our new home, Wenchi, found everyone in prime form. We rose by moonlight punctually at 5 o'clock and were soon on our way. The road was as wide as Piccadilly, and went through more variegated scenery than we had before, mostly open with bits of forest at times. I actually saw some bracken-like fern at one point. There were also quite a number and variety of flowers, a small bright blue kind of convolvolus, a pink one long stemmed rather like a rose, a pale violet one something between a sweetpea and a large violet, and a big yellow mallow affair. After this happy first hour's walk in the cool dawn we came upon a huge group of the natives working on the road; they were stripped to the waist and wielding pickaxes and looked like demons in Dante's Inferno. They gave way to let us pass while the Chiefs (Tekiman himself included) rose from their stools to greet us, which compliment we returned and after a few moments we proceeded on as quickly as possible. After several small clean villages which pleased D. no end we got into our hammocks about 8.30, and jogged along at a good pace with the little headman striding ahead, and bursting with pride in carrying the Union Jack over his shoulder. At Nkwansia about 4 miles from Wenchi, I was made to get out of my hammock and look at Wenchi on the hill beyond the next stretch of road. (Moses pointing out the Promised Land could hardly have felt more important than both Moussa and David himself did at that moment!) We inspected the rest-house, spoke to the Chief, thanked the music-makers who this time included a large melodeon and a squeegee band, directing them not to follow us too far as otherwise they would have been impossible to dispose of.

A quick passage for the next hour through more and more open country, with the road rising all the time, and we found ourselves welcomed by a positively regal reception both horse and foot.

Down the hill from the Zongo streamed a kaleidescopic crowd of men and boys heralded by two escort police from the prison who, with Moussa, then walked beside us to keep the throng from coming too close as we reclined in our litters. Hausas, Wangaras, Moshis, Fulanis, Ashantis, and others blaring all kinds of musical instruments, plus wonderful Chiefs in litters or on horseback, (their stools carried by boys on their heads) with umbrellas of state and other kingly paraphernalia. The caparisoned horses were covered with trappings of leather, silver work, and embroidered cloths, while their riders in voluminous flying robes and swathed head dresses sat in their high saddles also marvellously decorated. The Jimini Chief was an enormously tall North country man dressed in bright blue gallabeyah with a large hat topped with leather and a corner of it made entirely of brown ostrich feathers looking like a period

Paris fashion plate.

After passing the market we turned up an avenue of young flamboyant trees quite big although only planted last year, past the Court house where my lord dispenses justice, and then came to a final show of red and yellow Barbadoes pride in front of our first home together.

It is a low bungalow raised off the ground with a garden of flowers and fruit trees, a tennis court, and behind it the kitchen and servants quarters—beyond them is a flat green oblong space on one side of which is the prison and the orderlies and prison officers huts; at the far end nearer the actual village of Wenchi (which lies out of sight below the curve of the hill) is the rest-house for guests who may be visiting the District. Mr. Wood who has been in charge during David's absence met us there as he had got lunch ready for us. It was nearing midday by then, so we had done the 21 miles from Tekiman in reasonable time.

After luncheon D. showed me round the whole lay-out, and by the time we re-entered our own house the verandah and rooms were littered with boxes, baths, bags of bedding and, in fact, everything that we had either brought out by sea, or accumulated since disembarking on the Coast. I soon set to with the boys unpacking and selecting the necessary items for at least the next 24 hours, but it was difficult to concentrate on the task as the view to the North was simply wonderful with blue hills far in the distance rising above great plains of open country, and considerable stretches of forest. It only needed water, either sea or loch or river, to content me; one does miss that if used to it during one's young life, particularly after Scotland. All the afternoon carriers loads were being dumped around us, and by the time it was dark enough order had emerged to enable us to rest, have our baths, and change for dinner.

David and Mr. Wood were busy all this time handing and taking over the station, with all the District papers, cases pending, and general information about the last 5 months work and results. We were excorted over to the rest-house by Moussa with a lantern, and I admit that I rather thankfully sat down to be entertained and enjoy normal life. Our host is a tall young man perhaps 27 years old with an outspoken manner, rather judicial and very orderly, fond of housekeeping and music, road-making and intelligent conversation. He was a very good host, and gave us a most excellent meal. For anyone looking from the dark African night into the lighted rest-house dining-room across the wide verandah, the picture of three white people, the men in white mess jackets with bright yellow cummerbunds and I in a cool white dress, must have looked unexpectedly pleasant; it certainly was pleasant to us and we finally parted at 10.30 p.m. having had this almost European dinner party with records of Wagner and Beethoven's Moonlight Sonata playing as an accompaniment to our final evening of the journey from Scotland to our new African life.

# CHAPTER II

# Life at H.Q.

The first ten days of our new 'bush' life have passed so quickly that I never realized we were almost at the end of August until today; it is only three days to David's birthday on September 1st which I'll have to celebrate somehow.

It has all been most exciting for me as I had to be shown the village, the court, prison, and some of the outlying farms, as well as the difference between the North Country Zongos and the Ashanti sections of Wenchi itself. And then there were the names of the principal chiefs to be learnt, the names and duties of our own establishment, the police, and the hammock boys, gardeners, works men, and of course full details of Osman, the Head Clerk and his family.

Osman is a very intelligent Coast Native, who is responsible for all the office and Court work of the District under David, and acts as linguist (i.e. interpreter) for he is good both in Twi and Hausa—with all that, add inspection of sanitation and road work, the registering of guns, the taxes if any—all of which, some weeks, can keep both Commissioner and Head Clerk rather closely to H.Q.

My own job has been to arrange the house, do and check the unpacking and storing of all our foodstuffs, order meals and allot the responsible posts, while keeping an eye on the Jiminis who are building an extension of a bath and a bedroom for us at an angle to the existing house. (No plumbing of course, and the bath water is all brought up in tins filled daily by the prisoners.) Early rising here, where early bed naturally obtains, is quite easy with hours of daylight static from 6-6 and we have fruit and early tea on the verandah in our pyjamas, and set the gardeners their respective tasks before dressing ourselves; their hours or work are 6-11, and 1 to 5. Ths grass is cut by hand, the hammock boys squatting on the ground and using 'machetes' rather like kitchen choppers only with longer, narrower, blades. Mr. Wood from whom we took over was not keen on gardens; he asked me if the Barbadoes Pride were nasturtiums and said he didn't like flowers or grass, but just liked stones round a house—perhaps this was to discourage snakes and insects?— I thought a cemetery would suit him splendidly.

Moussa, the orderly, is most helpful and considerate. When I tried to help him put away stores on shelves, he politely but firmly declined to allow me to exert myself 'Missus not work'. Despite the 'Missus' I am generally spoken to as 'Sir', 'Yassah' and 'No Sah'. Rather quaint. Besides him our staff consists of ali the cook, Kudugu the cook's mate, Mama aged 16, valet, butler and houseboy, Tani, my maid and under housemaid, aged 13, Bawi about 10, who helps or gets in the way of everybody plus about a dozen men who are hammock or garden boys as circumstances dictate.

Most days we go out for a walk in the town with Ahmedu, the police sergeant, and Moussa, to see the sights; I was at first, evidently 'the sight', from the opposite point of view as the orderlies had hard work to keep a large following of interested spectators at a respectful distance! The market is fascinating and kaleidescopic as regards colour. There are 4 long, open, arcades made of plam tree trunks, roofed with palm thatch and under or beside these shelters were people buying and selling. There are about 8,000 mixed inhabitants in Wenchi, mostly Mahommedans except for the pagan Ashantis. There are Mosques that look like glorified sand castles in colour if not in shape, and the Mallams call to prayers at the acceptable hours. The slaughter house and butchers open market are the only European built buildings in the town and are very neat. Sometimes we meet Ansah the town clerk, a thin, nervous little man, who takes notes down in a small book at David's peremptory dictation. 'Why isn't this house built?', pointing to a collection of what looked like sticks—'Who does it belong to?'—'Get the man and bring him to court tomorrow'. 'Has so-and-so paid his rent for that house'—'No'. 'Bring him also to court tomorrow. Make a note of that'.

One day we espied a lean, little, mare with a foal, and Moussa tried to see if he could get the two for £4, and was despatched later with a box of sardines as a bribing prelude to a bargain—'Set a sardine to catch a horse!'; but he had no luck. An hour or so of this kind of thing and we were dead beat and moved homewards to retire to long chairs, a lime drink for me and something a little stronger for David. I must add here that during the first few days of our arrival we were 'dashed', 3 sheep, 300 eggs, 20 fowls and 50 yams! I daresay some of the eggs will hardly qualify for the new laid ticket of merit!

The Omanhin, the Mohammedan chiefs, and Osman, have all been to pay their respects; we were greatly amused by Osman who informed us with gravity that his wife's new baby had died two or three days before but, when sympathised with by David, only said with a happy smile 'Soon get another, Sah!' A Zongo chief 'dashed' some white pigeons, and also a few good breeding fowls; we might even grow some chickens ourselves. Lost sheep and donkeys are driven or carried up from the village and put into a small pound behind the prison; from there they have to be ransomed by payment of 1/- which is solemnly entered in the office accounts as 'Sundry building account!'—All these things, and one's own letter writing, ordering meals, and clipping the small shrubs and trees—keep me busy when alone.

David of course works at the Courthouse for 4 or 5 hours every day ironing out the District reports and programmes of work with Osman, as well as being on the Bench adjudicating land cases, giving a verdict on criminal ones, and generally being on tap when required.

Unlike most of the Ashanti chiefs, our local ruler is not necessarily a fetish worshipper, as this amusing letter will show. It is one written to David last January before he left on leave, but having said he hoped to return with a wife to whom he was already affianced.

*Letter from Ashanti Omanhin*
To His Worship, The Acting District Commissioner, Wenchi.
Kind Sir,
I have the honour most respectfully to write this calling your attention that I am in need of Cartridge and as such I should

be very much thankful to you for bringing me some when you return back from Home.

In fact your going home on leave has caused us a great deal of regret, by consideration I have found out that you are the man fit for this place, the construction of the streets of Zongo and other works have carried the name of Wenchi to far away and we are proud of it. Hence myself, sub chiefs, that of Zongo and neighbouring villages are praying that the All Father Mother God may bless you and protect you from all danger and be back amongst us with your wife through Christ our Lord. Amen!

I have the honour to be, Sir, Yours obedinetly,

OMANHIN OF WENCHI.

Whether pagans or Christians the Ashantis are extremly loyal to the British Government, which is publicly recognised by the fact that the W.A.F.F. battalion normally based on Coomassie has gone by sea to East Africa to fight there, leaving us with only a skeleton H.Q. and the usual Police guards at isolated District H.Qs. as in peacetime. Our French Ivory Coast neighbours have the same feelings about the war, and their local Provincial Commisioner at Bontuku has just sent us a letter to that effect and a large welcome basket of oranges.

As to village government, the local king or Omanhin rules his area under Ashanti custom tempered by or approved by the British Law while the Northern tribes in their own expatriate part of the villages come under British Law if need be, though as a rule they dwell quietly and according to Ashanti local customs.

Here, and in both Asia and most of Africa, the uneducated peoples make their complaints through public writers who are a recognised medium and receive pay for the work.

About twice a week we end up with a quick half hour or more getting the little farms nearest to the house beaten out on the chance of bagging a bushfowl (fakara) for tomorrow's lunch: these are the local partridges, very shy, very fast-flying, and very toothsome to eat! We both take our guns with three or four hammock boys plus Moussa to drive through the long grass: this has its difficulties what with ticks, and briars, and even snakes (one evening there was a large puffadder dislodged and killed,) but although I generally missed, and indeed have only killed two to date, a bag of two to four was generally brought home. Later on when the bustards begin to migrate, there will be more chances of what Moussa and the boys call 'meat' (this includes waterbuck, duikers, guinea fowl, green pigeons, and in fact anything that can be regarded as edible food).

The evening bath and change before dinner is often embellished by a wonderful last moment view especially with a moon following on the sunset. Tonight's sunset, for example, was marvellous, the glow perfect, making the Eastern sky a lovely blue against which clean white cumulus clouds floated. The flamboyant trees and a tamarisk tree stood clear and feathery against an all yellow sky with great pink rays radiating from it, while a silver moon sailed in the pink light. Then it all deepened, backed by dark hills silhouetted against a glaring orange curtain.

I forgot to say that soon after our arrival Hankuri also turned up. He is David's delightful dog who had been looked after by the Doctor at Kintampo while his master was away marrying me.

He is a big white mongrel, most like a large smooth West Highland terrier; his name means 'gracious pardon' or 'loving kindness', I'm told, and at present he is having ticks and other foreign bodies removed from his ears by Mama. 'Beef not live soon!' We feel quite complete now our dog has come but the poor doctor wrote a pathetic letter saying how sorry he was to lose him.

Hankuri didn't take long to settle down again, and already he is backwards and forwards to the village or the Court where he was always popular and everybody's friend. It amuses him to lie and watch Nubila, a butcher's assistant and as strong as the village blacksmith, who has joined us as our washerman; believe it or not, this new recruit has the most delicate touch, and deals with all our clothes as if they were gossamer.

The other morning, I suddenly heard great giggles coming from the unfinished bathroom; Mama and Tani were getting David's bath ready and the former had nearly stepped on a small snake. By the time I had come in to see what the joke was, the snake was still writhing though Mama had pretty well bashed its head in. I did not know if it was poisonous or not but one usually concluded the former. I then had the fun of looking at myself in a real mirror just arrived from Sunyani; up to now I've only had a small hand one (David's shaving glass) and I wanted to see if I had grown!

Outside the Jiminis were completing the demolition of the boys' old houses and putting up new ones. They came about 8 a.m. complete with orchestra, 'music while you work'. The procession wandered across the compound, the leader shaking a small sack of beans. There were 2 drums thumped by hand and 3 musical instruments of native construction. These were like small portable pianos played with little hammers. The musical result is a bit monotonous but not unpleasant to listen or work to. Shakey-akey, thumpety-thump and tinkle-inkle went on steadily for all the world like a non-stop downpour of rain, accompanied by a good deal of jabbering, laughing, and beating of the earth with poles. Then the framework of the houses go up and the playing is varied by a little step dancing. One man stepped out and did a 'pas-seul' pirouetting, jumping, skipping, and throwing his legs about while a very cheery fellow slapped a small drum with his hands and gyrated slowly round at the same time.

One of the nightly things that always intrigues me is the report by the corporal as to prison security and village be-haviour.—For example 'Fulani live for prison' means that one of the policemen was on guard, or 'no trouble village tonight' confirms that a stiff warning was given them as there were bands and shouts after 9.30 last evening.

Our fowl run was raided recently by two leopards who took our one good English cock, and a hen—a sad loss. Ali sat up the following night, but alas! they came this time to the gaoler's house and shed, retiring with his pet monkey and one of his hens! All animals including Hankuri were kept in after dark for some time, and the fowl runs and pigeon-cote safeguarded. In a small village near Tekiman about the same week a girl aged 12 was taken from an isolated house where she lived with her father; was it a were-leopard as was the local belief in Burmah when D. was there?

August 31st. A huge bag of mail has arrived. The reading of it makes us feel very far away from and out of the war. The news 4 or 5 weeks old, at least, when we get it. I opened 14 Times, a Spectator, Truth, Saturday Review, Observer and Bystander, off which I skimmed the cream and read about fighting the Bulgarians, and how all the allies were contributing to a force at Salonika. On the lighter side Ali is enchanted with the newly arrived cooking utensils, pots, pans, a potato masher, etc., also a 'flying pan!' He'll be able to make 'chicken cutlegs', and all kinds of good things.

September 1st. David's birthday. We had an early morning bushfowl shoot, the nearest equivalent to the opening partridge season. My bag was 0 and David's 7 and a green pigeon, but we lost 3 bushfowl irrevocably in the long grass. This all took place between 6.40 and 8.35. We bagged a woman as well, selling bananas on the road on the way home which must not be done as the market was built for that purpose, so she and 3 other accomplices were hauled along with us and left in charge of Osman to be sent down to the court for fining later. David got a few presents at the breakfast table, and also in the afternoon a parcel was found on his chair on the verandah. He opened it and drew forth a long raw, white cow's tail evidently just cut off. He thought it might be a joke in poor taste on Mama's part and hailed him wondering if he ought to be angry or not. However Mama after one shy laugh said it was a birthday present fro Mas'r to make a fly-whisk of as David had said some time ago he wanted a white fly-whisk!, and Mama had got the tail off a newly killed cow in the market today. So David thanked him and told him to hang it up to dry.

September 3. Days seem to be so dateless when time hardly matters. I often forget when it is Sunday and I was quite surprised to find we had been out with our guns today when I came to write my diary in the evening. No wonder I met a mad cow when breaking the Sabbath! We were walking home with 5 bushfowl to David's gun and saw some cattle being driven ahead. Suddenly we heard Moussa saying behind us ' 'Bad cow, bad cow' and I looked to my right and saw a dun, horned, cow running in the bush and coming straight for me apparently very mad. Instinctively I darted across the road, the brute after me, and got behind a small dead tree for safety while he came slap at me and just shaved me. I fled round the tree and doubled back to the road again but tripped and fell headlong in the grass quite expecting the next moment to feel the beast's horns ploughing my back. Somehow I picked myself up and David was beside me in an instant, the cow having missed me and gone into the bush. We climbed a tree and Moussa went off to fetch David's elephant gun as we were quite near home. We examined our guns as David and Moussa, who was carrying my gun, had inadvertently banged them against each other with the idea of stopping the cow from pursuing me. I felt a bit shaky as I'd been missed by an inch or so! We walked home in the gathering dusk, expecting the animal to spring out of the bush at every step. By this time, Moussa having been to the house, Mama and Ali with lanterns, and the police corporal with umbrellas (for rain was coming on) all came tearing along to meet us and we weren't sorry to reach the compound, surrounded by our retainers. David insisted on my having a whisky and soda—about the first in my life—and then a hot bath restored my shattered frame which had only suffered bruises and a stiff arm. The gun barrels were a bit dented, but not badly as we proved next day after careful examination.

A few days ago we had heard drums beating after tea, so went for a walk with Moussa in the town and saw the end of a wedding. It was the last day before the bride and groom go to live together. The company formed a circle all round and watched the antics of the performers. These were very funny. A man would jump into the middle of the group and twist his legs about and another rushed in with a little leather whip and pretended to beat people and two men played tom-toms while small girls and a few older ones sang a kind of chorus wriggling slowly round just moving their feet and hands. The bride and bridegroom sat on chairs a little apart, the bridegroom with a new shawl all over him and white canvas shoes showing beneath it. The bride in a gay cloth, her face and shoulders covered with a dark blue veil and silver bangles on her wrists and arms. The men made awful faces and looked killingly funny jumping, leaping, stamping and grimacing. I was rooted to the spot with fascination till ominous signs in the skies portended a rain-storm and sent us scurrying home.

Another Sunday, on which the Jiminis being Moslems naturally worked, they had the boys' new houses to finish; so we took the pathephone out to give them a treat in the shape of a tune or two. We turned on 'Hitchy Koo' and they all came crowding round, looking inside the box, very puzzled to know where the sound came from, still more so when we put on a Harry Lauder song and he started by laughing. That set them off. A tall woman stepped out in front and began posturing and dancing in front of the pathephone with a profoundly grave expression on her face and an entire absence of self-consciousness or embarrassment. It was marvellous the way she picked up the time of the tune, listening for a minute proceeding to move her feer and arms in perfect unison. I was as tickled as Jock of the song! After this interlude they returned to work, mixing the clay for the walls. The men were tramping about and paddling on great mud heaps mixed with water and earth which made their feet and legs gloriously messy. This mixture is called 'swish'.

We came in and had church ourselves. The pathephone had come with us and produced 'Old 100' and 'Lead Kindly Light' so with the service we read, it sounded just like a proper church. After that the Sunday roast beef of Ashanti, otherwise groundnut, a 5 course meal in itself, which engendered an after heavy luncheon calm!

September 4th. None the worse of yesterday; just as well as Mr. Ross, the Provincial Commissioner, and Dr. Duff were arriving on a visit of inspection from Sunyani, about 35 miles away. We supplied them with lunch. They are putting up at the rest-house. The men shot in the evening and Mr. Ross gave us a very good dinner at the rest-house where we were greatly amused by his grey parrot which is vocal, but was mute in our presence, Just as well perhaps, as I believe his language was not exactly that of a church conference. Anyhow he did his parlour trick of permitting his master to lay him on his back on the table, where he lay stiff and still with his legs in the air and Mr. Ross pretended to carve him up with a knife and fork. Mr. Ross began life in the training ship 'Worcester' from which he went to sea, and was round the Horn three times in square-rigged ships.

The visitors leave tomorrow but as we are going on trek shortly to Sikassiko on the Ivory Coast border, we will see them again for we intend to return via Sunyani. Sikassiko in our district is only 10 miles from Bontuku, and the plan is for us to visit that place, and then escort M. Prouteaux, the French

Commissioner, back with us to Sunyani. I must rub up my French as we hear M. Prouteaux speaks no English.

David as it happens went as far as Nkwansia with Mr. Ross next day so I was alone, but the boys and Moussa do everything they can and make things pleasant for me. I watched the boys having a washing day, three of them sitting in the compound with a tin bath and enamelled basin, sheets and pillow cases and clothes floating in the breeze around them. Nubila has constituted himself head washerman. It was curious to see his great fists handling some of my frailer garments. I had thought when it came to ironing I would do these myself rather than let Mama and Nubila slam a heavy box iron down on them, but on comparing a silk shirt done by Mama and one done by myself I found he got first prize easily.

September 8th. A few fairly uneventful days have passed though something interesting or amusing is always happening. Tonight it was bright moonlight and it roused the female population to shriek and sing and yell monotonous choruses. The moon seems to have the same effect on these people as it has on impressionable dogs. Their innumberable Dane guns were fired off at intervals of about 5 minutes and drums were beaten, so David in a great rage got up from bed, as we had gone there early, and called Mama to tell the corporal to go and stop the jamboree. Drumming is not allowed at night without a pass from the Commissioner. These particular drums were about 2 miles off and sounded quite close. The noise carries absolutely miles on a still night, up to 20 or even more. After some time had elapsed the drumming ceased, the firing of salvos stopped and even the 'bits of Ashanti fluff' desisted from their melancholy caterwauling and we were able to sleep in peace.

During the day we had been in the town having walked round by the prison which David inspected, and then on by the slaughterhouse, cattle market and Hausa and Wangara Zongos (encampment or section of the same race). There was a lot of cattle, speckled, dun and brown and the young bloods of the place were having a canter on their little 'dokis' (horses) fairly flying along at top speed, voluminously clad and white-turbanded. The costumes are intriguing. The children often have only a simple string of beads round their middles and work up to a gaily patterned cotton cloth often tied at the back of the neck, then to embroidered loose trousers, 2 or 3 white or blue cotton robes and head swathings round mouth, chin and throat, very often with a saucy, straw hat on top of it all.

September 11th. Today we have left for 'bush' and expect to be away from headquarters between 2 and 3 weeks. We were called at 6 a.m. and after breakfast there was a great to-do, sending off carriers, putting things away in the house, and giving orders all round. I sat amid the debris reading Neil Munro's 'Lost Pibroch' meanwhile. At last we got under way at a quarter to eight, but had only a short 8½ mile march to Tainsu so I walked all but the last mile; and got there at 10.20. We missed Hankuri soon after starting so two boys had to go back for him and found him gallivanting about the town; he was led back by his gaolers, excited, hot and with yards of tongue hanging out.

Tainsu is quite near the river Tain, a broad, sluggish stream crossed by a dug-out as ferry. We sat on a fallen tree above the ferry and watched passengers crossing, some of whom were stopped by David and their loads examined, tales having been heard of powder being smuggled into French country which is forbidden: however it was a case of 'pass friends, all's well'. The rest-house is right on the river bank. A platform of earth with a thatched roof on poles is where we take our meals. We dozed and read, did a Hausa lesson for my benefit and turned in early, a great yellow moon making it very light so I slept rather badly. Horrible birds made the night hideous by their disgusting noises. Crow pheasants go Coo-hoo-hoo-hoo and answer one another in deep, mocking tones, bushfowl cackle madly and other birds, animals and insects all take part in the great African orchestra. The noisiest is the hyrax who begins on a reasonably low note and works up to a screeching crescendo. Mosquitos ping outside the nets over one's camp bed and long to suck one's blood, especially good fresh stuff like mine and given any chance, like 'the stag at eve, drink their fill'.

Usual early start next day after morning hubbub of striking camp. We crossed the Tain in a dug-out and I walked for 2 hours and took to my hammock just short of Nsokor at which village we debated the burning question of stopping there for luncheon or pressing on to Menge, our destination. As it was only 10.30 we decided to press on. Ali is not at all well and has had fever and now, with a bad knee and swollen hand he looks very miserable. But he's game and carries on. We walked along a gravelly, sandy, roadway bordered by trees and scrubby orchard trees. It looked like good 'hunting' country and we kept thinking bits of trees were heads and horns looking at us out of the long grass. Moussa was on ahead with our guns anyhow, while Hankuri panted after us. I took him into my hammock once, but five minutes there together satisfied both of us as we preferred our own room to our joint company!

At Nsokor the village turned out and beat large drums with deafening insistency while two huge state umbrellas waved in the breeze and various hangers-on danced, shouted, ran ahead and alongside us. The same happened as we neared Menge where another cheery crowd met us and 'dashed' us eggs and yams. We were glad to relax in the rest-house of this pretty village after our lunch off the ubiquitous chicken and marma-lade omelette. The mallam called from the mosque which was like an ice cream pudding stuccoed with almond; these are the wooden gutterings that stick out from the sand-coloured walls. I was bitten by every available insect while we rested! We bestirred ourselves, had baths and changed at 3.30 and then went round the town for a walk accompanied by the two Chiefs of the two parts of the town and one of the linguists. The people were all dancing round the mosque, the men cutting extraordinary capers, the women and girls shuffling along with heads bent down, coloured handkershiefs or cowtail flywhisks in their hands. The 'band' looked quite demented thumping on their drums or keeping back the small fry with whips and much pushing, very like policemen keeping back a scrum at home. The noise, dust, and hot smell in the air made it all rather exhausting. As a rest David heard a complaint from a chief, and we then went 'home' to play the gramophone and watch a stormy sunset behind the hills which transformed itself into a fierce thunder, lightning and rainstorm about 10 o'clock, when the roof leaked, David's bed had to be moved, and I heard hyenas howling. Just a 'wee opera' as a friend once described kittens playing! The storm subsided and we slept.

Up at 6.30 and off to Debibi, some 14 miles away. We are in Jaman country since leaving Tainsu and the people are different with a language of their own. It rained a good deal and we tramped along for 2 hours under a large carriage umbrella. We went through one village, Nomassa, and though dark and stormy looking, a mirthful crowd came running out to meet us down a long, steep, hill which led up to the village. These danced and sang, and played their primitive musical instruments. Two or three men jumped in the air, stamped on the ground and twiddled their toes, while a little boy pranced ahead waving artistically, a bunch of green leaves in one hand and red in the other. Another looked very funny wearing an embroidered pill box on his head, a cloth round his small frame and carried an umbrella. It started to pour so we hastily had a native hut cleared out and sat down there for an hour while people crowded around, and the hammocks and boys arrived, everything wet; David cursing, and I sitting like Patience on a deck chair amid the debris. Off again when the rain stopped still accompanied by the inhabitants probably rejoicing as much to see us go as arrive. One delightful chap was clean off his dot and rushed from side to side of the road, tearing through the long grass and dragging off branches of trees which he chucked about, from sheer 'joie de vivre' I suppose. I read 'The Lunatic at Large' in my hammock during the last few miles of our march which was appropriate to the foregoing, and walked to within a mile of our destination, Debibi, where the chief borne in a litter met us. His umbrella bearer carrying a vast red and yellow 'parapluie' ran alongside David's hammock trying to hold it over him; it got caught up in a bush once which delayed the poor man for some minutes to his great distress and my unholy joy!

Debibi is a typical big Jaman village, all the houses in a clump together with the main road running through it and an enormous baobab tree in the middle, huge gnarled roots sticking out of the ground all round and creepers hanging down from it. We seemed to be accompanied by the entire population to the rest-house. David thinks they are displaying unusual activity in the entertainment line owing to my presence! The rest-house is of the old Ashanti type, a square open courtyard enclosed by 3 or 4 small rooms open in front, all except the bedroom which has a wall with kind of portholes in it. It is going to be pulled down tomorrow and a new type one put up, 2 rooms with a wide verandah all round, the whole covered by a thatched roof. Drastic methods obtain here. David found the road blocked by the beginnings of a house at a small village near Wenchi, so after asking how the people had dared to build it to sprawl half over the road, without sound of trumpets he pushed the walls down flat with his stick like those of Jericho and passed on! Ali and Mama had already arrived at Debibi, as had also 'dashed' chickens, of which we are sending back three or four to Wenchi to 'make eggs', to use English as she is spoken. Water is scarce here but we got baths and had some boiled for drinking. Tani then decorated the roof with the clothes we had taken off; it was rather comical to see all manner of intimate garments taking the air to dry.

As breakfast had been eaten at 6 a.m. we were pretty hungry for lunch after 1 o'clock. Never did onion omelette, roast guineafowl and tinned pears taste so good. Long chairs and rest followed, accompanied by a Hausa lesson. In the middle of translating, 'Who told you the news?' David drew my attention to a large frog hopping over the sandy ground straight towards us. What looked like a long piece of grass was waving behind it. It was a bright green snake. David seized part of the framework of the loggia, a long pole which came conveniently away in his hand to dispatch the snake with. The snake, anticipating danger, sat up and stared at him, so I called Mama and Bawi who dashed into the fray with more long poles and it was killed by a bash on the head. This is only the third snake I have seen since I arrived in West Africa.

Half the male population appeared after our 4 o'clock cup of tea and were turned on to breaking down old buildings on the rest-house site; pretty well every trace was removed in half an hour and the new rest-house site marked out with posts. We directed operations from our 'sit-down sticks', (shooting sticks) very convenient seats on these occasions. The Jamans are kindly, simple, souls very brown and very undressed, just a fore and aft cloth on; they almost melt into their background.

September 14th. Another 6.30 start and away with us on our trek to Sikassiko. We did about 10 or 11 miles on foot, passing only one village called Duadaso, rather a large, squalid, depressing place, full of very black old men and pigs to match. There were plenty of goats and sheep too. A bit further on there was another part of the same village, more prosperous looking and cleaner. Moussa was left behind to instruct the aged chief and his people to clean up and tidy the less attractive portion of Duadaso. The scenery was slightly more diverse today, with views of hills and plenty of farms, as we got near Sikassiko where the usual warm welcome met us at 10.30. A jingle-jangle, squeegee band preceded us and a large following walked beside our hammocks, some rather repulsive old women prancing and clapping their hands and waving their arms accompanied by children of both sexes. All very jolly anyhow. They left us at the rest-house, a great big one, full of scorpions, hornets and white ants. The latter accounted last year for a guncase, pair of pyjamas and a flannel blazer of David's. Of the pyjamas the only bit the white ants couldn't stomach was the cord. David had thrown the pyjamas on the ground the night before and found only the cord in the morning!

This place was a military station between 1896 and 1906 and three white officers lived here and kept a company of W.A.F.Fs. going. The French country is only about 2 miles away. Poor Ali is in great pain with hand and arm all swollen up. We think of sending him on to Sunyani in David's hammock to see the doctor but it is 75 miles away, and a 3 or 4 day journey. I bathed them in hot water and put on a bandage and sling made out of a small tablecloth and tried to make it comfortable. Ali told us the chief here had a medicine for it as he had often seen and cured like swellings before, so we are going to let him try it; then on Saturday if it is no better we will send him to Sunyani. It was very hot and we had baths and changed before lunch. Water is bad and very scarce here. Our baths were filled with most unattractive warm water of pea soup colour and of about the same consistency. This being the rainy season is about the best time for water too, so at the worst time it must be almost solid mud.

After tea we walked downhill to the little cemetery enclosed by a thicket of trees and containing three pathetic graves. The nameless one is of a native officer, and two English ones are of Captain Osborne Fraser who died in 1899 and Lieut. Martin in 1905. We went through the town and had a talk to some of the elder brethern assembled under a tree, and then stopping some men from digging a grave in the middle of the street. After that David nosed around the outskirts to hunt out standing water, stagnant pools, and unweeded patches of overgrown ground and so on. Finally we proceeded to the Jimini settlement which was very satisfactory and picturesque. Several long open air looms were being worked in a clear sandy space; the deep blue Hausa cloth is dyed locally, I think. Little round houses like beehives were where corn is stored. There were lots of goats and pi-dogs who came out to insult Hankuri, which we drove off with sticks and stones. We commanded a fallen tree of great size lying across the main road to Bontuku to be removed. Bontuku is 10 miles away in the Ivory Coast and we visit it tomorrow. The French had sent us a great treat in the shape of cabbage which, as Ali is hors de combat, Kudugu, the cook's mate, surpassed himself in serving up with dinner. This rest-house is the old mess and captain's house, supposed nowadays to be haunted, but I don't know who by.

David overheard the boys discussing white women in general and me in particular. He heard one say 'White women are very curious', and Moussa answered, 'This one is not a woman, she is a girl and she plays!' Undisturbed by nothing worse than mosquitos pinging around the nets and thirsting for our blood, we slept soundly.

# CHAPTER III

# Visit to Bontuku

September 15th

Since our first arrival on the Coast over 6 weeks ago we had not required to rig ourselves out in anything smart, but today was different as we were paying an official call on the French Commissioner at Bontuku. Eight o'clock therefore saw us leaving by hammock (not walking) in full dress, myself in quite a decent white dress and general turnout while David had his best white uniform, gold buttons, Wellington boots, and usual West Coast official details. It was gloriously cool, misty, and remained almost without rain all day.

Moussa and Osman were left behind to tidy up the town and we took Sergeant Ahmedu and Mama, both riding bicycles.— The frontier is only about 2 miles away, the road good and broad, but the Tain river which is here the frontier was very full, and we were lucky to get across dry—in fact the hammock men who carried us only just kept us above the waterline, they themselves being up to their waists! A bridge is not really necessary when there are no vehicles, and (unless flooded) not enough water to prevent cattle or humans passing.

On the French bank there was one Senegalese soldier with a note of welcome from the Commissioner; he turned and followed us back to the little frontier post in a small village which has a Customs Office in charge of a pale homely-looking Frenchman with 3 more soldiers—to all of whom we uttered a few platitudes before pushing on. There were a lot of monkeys skipping about on the roofs of houses; they are fetish monkeys fed by the villagers.

About half-past ten we arrived at Bontuku to be greeted by

Monsieur Prouteaux, the Senior Commissioner, and Monsieur Chaumel, his Assistant; the former a grizzled hair and moustached man of about 40, and the latter a modern looking French youth of perhaps 27 with a long elegant figure, a thin face, deep set eyes, very fair brushed back hair and a sloping forehead. Neither of them speak English; we conversed in French from the very beginning.

We had got out of our hammocks before meeting them outside the town, so after the exchange of greetings we all four entered the town together; I must say that I was tremendously impressed with it, not only by its atmosphere, its tidiness, and its curious air of a different world, but also by its history as one of the most important trading centres between Central Africa and the Coast. Being half way between Bamako the terminus of the French railway and the English one at Coomassie, Bontuku is well placed for trade as well as politically if allied needs have to be gone into.

The town is unbelievably different from the types seen in the Coast or in Ashanti; it is almost entirely Moorish (perhaps an Egyptian touch in it as well) with great big hard-baked sand and mud houses (all flat roofs), mosques, and narrow streets— there are no thatched roofs at all. The population is mainly Mahommedan, and it is the seat of the Almami, the spiritual chief of that part of the Ivory Coast. We met him coming to greet us almost at once, and David was able to exchange a few remarks about the war and our allied interests—which is important for he has great influence. A dignified, nice man.

This little digression over, our hosts conducted us through various quarters of the town in an absolute ear-racking din of noise for the inhabitants had now been let loose on us, and accompanied us everywhere; we had to shout to each other in order to get any conversation at all! We went inside one of these large houses, through a dark living-room, and then out on to the roof from where looking down we could see the gaily-coloured moving crowds beneath and beyond the town itself the green hills, for the place lies in a large cup between hills and forests in every direction. From another large house further on we got a bird's eye view of the dye-wells. They dye yarn and cloth here in large quantities—the colour is a deep kind of butcher's blue—of remarkable beauty, and the tall Wangara

35

and other tribesmen look particularly splendid in such robes.

Close to these wells is a broad avenue of flamboyant trees, some orange and limes in fruit were visible also. From all this, still pursued by the crowd with music fore and aft, we walked up a longish hill to the P.C. bungalow. This was set in a large well laid out compound with mangoes, Barbadoes pride, cactus's, crotons, and other shrubs planted in it. We seated ourselves on a piazza, the crowd having still accompanied us, but they dispersed after about 5 minutes, and we were offered 'aperitifs'. I chose a compound of vermouth and 'syrup', diluted with water which became a bright, orange-red, colour, and this I sipped, hoping I would remain upright. Lunch followed in an inner room, 7 courses, no less, and drinks 'en suite'. Thereafter I was presented with photographs of the town, a native leather satchel, a dancing stick decorated with leather and cowries and bits of leopard skin, and literally dozens of postage stamps as I had said something about collecting these.

We left at 3.15, laden with good things, David so much so, that with the jogging of the hammock he arrived back with a raging headache. A disturbed night followed as he felt the worse for wear, a storm came on and rain leaked on to my bed, necessitating a move, thunder rumbled incessantly. Hankuri rattled his chain and shook my bed (we have to tie him up at night for fear of hyenas) and as David says the rest-house is reputed to be haunted the astral spirits added to the night's disturbance. Anyhow we had for us, when on trek, 'a long lie', and only got up at 7. We have two sick men on our hands though Ali is no worse, but another boy has a frightfully swollen back and we only hope we get them to Sunyani for treatment by the Doctor.

A wonderful barbaric procession met us after breakfast when we went out. First a line of men carrying low Ashanti chairs studded all over with brass and gold nails arranged in patterns, then the young king of Wirime and the old prince carried on men's heads in litters which are long crib-like baskets; over them were held gorgeous umbrellas, red, yellow, blue and white topped by a crescent moon, porcupine and snake ready to strike, I suppose, made of brass. Royalty descended from their litters and greeted us by shaking hands. The young King was an enormous man of about 27 at a guess, who wore a red robe and sandals, the robe all hung round with mounted lions claws, bits of leopard skin and gold and a headdress composed in like fashion. The old prince is about 70 and last year when ill got some quinine from David which was efficacious, so he thinks David saved his life and is very fond of him in consequence. This company then went to the court to hear cases, accompanied thither by 'the band' which consisted of native drums, carried on men's heads, and beaten vigorously, hand bells and other unknown, music-making, quantities. I looked into our chopbox and made out a menu for M. Prouteaux's dinner tonight, which later we composed in our best French for his benefit. Despite the Tain's flood he arrived safely at 6 o'clock amid much noise, we having arranged for a sort of triumphal procession 'pour lui faire honneur'. The dinner, and French conversation having passed off successfully, we retired to bed early in view of the morrow's start.

When we got under way at 7 a.m. next morning we looked quite 'formidable', as our ranks were swollen by the French carriers, clerk, hammock boys and orderly, also by a corporal and two soldiers sent up from Sunyani as an escort. We had a short, 13 mile, day to Sekatea, but went through 2 or 3 villages stopping at one called Drobo for a short time where there was a fine old king with a retinue carrying the usual state umbrella, drums and swords; there M. Prouteaux was offered what looked like a mad bull tied up, but he refused this politely while we graciously accepted yams, chickens and eggs as being more useful. On reaching Sekatea we lunched in a loggia outside the rest-house, then retiring to rest, after which the two commissioners went for a walk round the village while a sheep, presented here to the Frenchman, bleated all afternoon while tied to a post. I was relieved when the carriers took it away, I fear, to have the pleasure of 'chopping' him and having a good blow-out. We sat in a little circle of light for dinner surrounded by dense outer darkness. Showers of insects descended and soon the table was covered with small, medium and large ants, flies of every description and other insect world specimens. I copied an owl with my clasped hands and got one to answer me. Bed at the early hour of 8.30.

Off at 6.40 a.m., next day, on our 20 miles march to Pulliano, our last sleeping place in David's district. It was lovely and cool, travelling was pleasant, and the only snag was when brought to a halt by the Tain which was again very high and flooding the land. Uusually it can almost be jumped, today it was a deep, brown, turgid river, in fact we heard that a hippopotamus was in it further down having come from the North. A small and coggly dugout awaited our pleasure, crewed by two natives. These paddled M.P., myself and Hankuri over, landing us in some nice, squelchy mud, the track being simply a secondary tributary. David and Moussa came next but the whole caval-cade had to be ferried over. Meantime Moussa was told off to escort me to where the road began again which he did by carrying me in his brawny arms, while he paddled cautiously along, almost up to his knees in water. I sat on a tree stump by the side of the now recognizable track, till everyone else arrived.

We got to a place called Fuamang at midday, and halted for lunch which we ate in a thatched shelter near a tree infested by weaver birds who chattered around their ball-like nests, and pulled off leaves and twigs and scattered them all over the the ground to show, I like to think, their disapproval of our presence. The villagers assembled under the spreading flam-boyant tree and the king or chief, having been dumped out of his litter and on to his throne, the usual impromptu pas-seuls and dances, executed by any inspired male or female taken that way, were performed for our edification. Travelling on, there-after, we first went through light forest with patches of marshy open savannah, ending up with proper Ashanti forest, rain falling heavily for nearly 2 hours, during which we followed a serpent-like, muddy track which wound in and out of the trees great tall ones with rope-like creepers hanging down and twisted round the trunks like snakes. There were ferns growing quite near the tops sometimes and it was extraordinary to see the number of dead trees, gaunt white skeletons stretching out bony shining limbs to the sky. Then we emerged into sunshine and long elephant grass and a broad, new red gravelly road stretching up in front of us to Pulliano. With our French guest leading the van in his hammock chair carried by 4 boys in red blouses (like the French man's 'blouse bleu') which give them the appreance of Japanese coolies, then David in his (he had walked the whole way except about an hour so that meant he had done 18 miles on his flat feet) and then me, followed by the 'tail', we cantered up hill into Pulliano to be met by an hilarious crowd, chiefs, litters, umbrellas through a broad clean and cheerful village to the rest-house.

The sun shone brightly after rain and the village is on top of a hill among elephant grass, a wide space some 7 miles by 2 amid the forest. We got here about 4 o'clock and had tea in the loggia as soon as it could be made, while sparrows and swallows imparted a home flavour by chirping and wheeling around. It really is wonderful the way these youthful domestics of ours walk 20 miles and at the end of it furnish the house, unpack china, glass and cutlery, cook and heat water for baths and a good deal else besides. Their work in headquarters appears light compared to that same service at home but the real test comes trekking in the bush, and our boys certainly shine like the stars of the firmament on these occasions. As we sat at tea up came a crowd with presents and Osman read out the list of 'dashes' from each chief and interpreted a little speech of thanks back to them. Then unpacking, baths, change, rest, dinner, and soon thereafter bed.

September 19th.

Our destination today was Berekum, 20 miles away. Having unbuttoned our eyes at 5.45, we were on the road an hour later and it was a real newly made highway running between waving elephant grass some 14 feet high. It was interesting to note the gradual transition back to real Ashanti country by which I mean, cocoa farms, forest and the mixture of new and old in villages. One part of the road was very pretty, simply masses of the trees called flame of the forest, dark green with bunches of brilliant red blossom. We passed through two villages 'en route', at the second of which a following accompanied us to Berekum, and young men made a joyful noise with a concertina, horns fashioned from those of cattle or elephants' tusks and drums. A new note was added to proceedings by the firing of Dane guns, long, old muzzle loaders. It was fun seeing the gunpowder being ladled down and then bang! bang! into the bush and a flame and blue smoke hanging among the greenery while the marksmen hurried on with their weapons to repeat the 'feu de joie' further on. Berekum has an important king so the din and noise increased 'pari passu' as we neared the place. A whole lot of little boys under the native Basle mission teacher lined the road, saluting, and singing, 'God Save the King'. Gun after gun went off, state umbrellas like huge gaily coloured toadstools could be seen flapping and waving in the distance. The umbrellas are very heavy to handle and the bearers of them shift their hands and keep them moving to take the weight off.

It was quite a triumphal entry into the town what with crowds of perspiring humanity, gunpowder smoke, dust, chairs borne aloft, stopping and shaking hands with the king, who directly we went on was bundled with lightning celerity into his litter and shot aloft on the heads of his men who cantered along near us in our hammocks. Berekum is in the Sunyani district, a clean, pretty little town of thatched houses and fine trees planted down the middle of the street. Mr. Ross had provided quarters for us at the Basle mission and our guest had the rest-house. The European missionaries have gone, the native one carries on. I was glad to sink into a chair in one of the rooms of the mission and take stock of my surroundings. There was a table, a cuckoo clock that didn't cuckoo, a sideboard, 2 religious pictures, 2 texts in Twi, 2 manufacturers calendars and a few photographs, one of our king and queen and family, reinforced by a white Spitz dog, circa 1913. It was very hot and after entertaining M. Prouteaux to a cold lunch we rested, despite the thumping and rolling of drums and the ting-ting like an impatient steamer's bell, and other noises 'off'.

I have not said a word about the war for a long time but Ashanti seems a 'far cry' from the fields of Flanders or Salonika; we get but scant news, and that only from belated newspapers. We are now in the third year of war and read of the French and ourselves pushing on in Flanders and France, the Italians capturing Gorizia from the Austrians, and Zeppelins being sent to bomb Britain. But it is some time since we had a mail and papers.

At 5 o'clock we took our guest a stroll in the town ending up under a big tree where the king was sitting under a state umbrella with a party of his elders and sword bearers round him, the latter sitting on low Ashanti stools holding up the gold topped emblems leading the approach to the throne. It made a splendid picture of regal, barbaric, magnificence. The great crowd around was like a dark wall; after a photograph was taken we spoke to the King through an interpreter and thanked him for his welcome. Then we shook hands. The King wore a magnificent cloth all hand-woven in multi-coloured square patches with lines between. It was all silk and as such cost about £15 to buy. Gold rings and ornaments adorned his person. He let me feel the stuff of his robe and express my admiration through Osman. This friendly court occasion over, we were quite glad to retire to our house and dine.

Next day has been a terrific one, as we left Berekum at 6.15 a.m. in order to arrive at Sunyani before luncheon—and it is a good 21 miles in all. Apart from that we knew that Ross would have laid on a really smart welcome to do honour to our ally, and timing therefore was important. Both David and M. Prouteaux were rigged out in full white uniforms and accoutrements, while I looked a regular jungle wallah in my old clothes, but we had a quiet comfortable journey, hammocking all the way, and an excellent road. Then nearing Sunyani about midday we were fairly bounced out of our hammocks by the blazing off of 50 or 60 Dane guns fired by lines of half-naked men on the side of the road, shooting off into the bush; the air was absolutely full of smoke and the smell of gunpowder.

Further on we passed the Chiefs and their suites sitting in their baskets on men's heads with lovely umbrellas over them, and gold topped swords of state held beside them. Then the sound of the Marseillaise was wafted on the breeze, and we came upon the Government School children lining the road waving French tricolour flags, singing lustily and very creditably. This they repeated 20 times, and finally we turned up a long avenue of flamboyant trees away from the town and up a hill towards the bungalows where Ross and Dr. Duff were waiting to receive us. On the way we passed through a Guard of Honour of the W.A.F.F., their bugler standing at the foot of a flagstaff where the Union Jack and the French flag flew together.

It really was a great reception that M. Prouteaux got, and when on entering Ross's bungalow he was handed a telegram from the Governor welcoming him to the Colony his cup of happiness ran over. Ross himself welcomed our visitor with a toast in champagne, after which we retired to the different bungalows for a wash and tidy up before meeting again 'chez' Ross who is host to us all; we were very ready for luncheon.

I think everyone must have been glad of a real laze this afternoon, and nothing happened until after a cup of tea we went to have a look at the fort which had been built after the 1900 show. The ramparts were now overgrown, as was the subterranean passage from the fort to the water supply (a lesson well learnt from the last war); today it is used for a prison. We were going further afield to look at gardens and new houses, but a terrific black cloud heralded a rapidly approaching storm so we made for the Dispensary instead. Actually the Doctor had just rushed off there as he saw an apprently lifeless man being carried into the hospital. He turned-out to be a local, about 30, who had tried to strangle himself and was at the last gasp but the doctor applied artificial respiration at once—which soon succeeded after which we heard groans and weird noises. He had a quarrel with his brother and really did try to strangle himself in the middle of it. We sat in the Dispensary talking to Mr. Ross, while the Doctor showed the Frenchman all the doings, and the hospital in full.

Today (21st September) is a real sort of half-holiday, and it gives M. Prouteaux time to think over all he has seen and done, while allowing Ross and my husband to discuss local politics, new jobs to be done, and (in David's case) opportunities for asking if there are any useful spare stores such as paint which he can have, or managing to get hold of them on the quiet as Sunyani is always well stocked. After luncheon and a short siesta, we all went for a long walk to the town past the hospital, the clerks' houses, and over a little stream to see the Ashanti section which was rather higher up. We looked into some of the local stores, Swanzys and others—but there was nothing to tempt one. After that along the Coomassie road to the Hausa Zongo, which here is small and not particularly good to look at but this is not a normal road from North to South, and gets few immigrants. There was a nice old Wangara buffer to whom we spoke a little, after which we inspected a new cattle kraal, the very good water supply, and then in the quickly falling shadows went back to our houses, our baths, and our dinner at Ross's bungalow.

The following day I started by walking down to the Court-

house and offices with David who was in grand form as he had
managed to collect wire, cement, a drum of distemper, another
of green paint, besides lots of seedlings and cuttings for our
gardens! Ali is now walking about in a cloth with his arm in a
sling, but the doctor says he must keep him back a day or two
when we leave tomorrow, and Tinorga much longer as he is
seriously ill with a kind of pleurisy. After luncheon we took the
tennis court measurements, and then Mr. Ross gave me a very
fine English hen out of his fowl run and quite a lot of vegetables
from his beautifully kept small kitchen garden; we can't exactly
be jealous, for Sunyani has existed for some fourteen years,
and Wenchi was only begun last year when David had it—
but it is splendid to have something to compare, and then to
try and equal for onself.

After tea we all went as it were officially to the school sports
which had been planned as a central demonstration which the
Chiefs and people of all kinds would attend, and so understand
this as an occasion for the allies, French and English to corrobo-
rate in meeting and approving of the visit. One or two bad
rain showers delayed the proceedings, but about 6.30 we
successfully reached the school grounds and sports arena where
a rather important King of Odumase had been specially posted
near the entrance so that our ally could meet and talk with him;
—the actual approach was through a gateway of freshly cut
palm leaves decorated with small tricolour flags!

After a band had once more given us the Marseillaise the
sports began. All the competitors were boys except one girl
called Maria. There were races of all kinds, egg and spoon,
sack, plus some jumping; but on that slippery ground jumping
was hardly possible without poles. Every event evoked roars of
laughter (countless falls!), and the tug of war most of all. At
the end I presented the prizes (the one girl got 3rd prize in
the egg and spoon race), and noticed that they all came up
very smartly and saluted with military precision. Then departure, which meant about 10 minutes of noise with 'national
anthems', eternal drumming, horn blowing, shouts, and
stampedes of young ones trying to keep up with us, or with the
Chiefs, or with themselves—but at last we Europeans did extract
ourselves and being met by our own boys with lanterns soon
found ourselves at peace, and very ready to change and dine

quietly.

Today September 23rd saw the break-up of the party, as we wanted to get back to Wenchi as soon as possible, while Mr. Ross had to accompany M. Prouteaux to Coomassie which meant quite a lot of receptions and fast trekking for them. We decided to leave first, so as to make it easier for the carriers not to mix up loads; to do that we dashed across to say goodbye to the others while still at breakfast. But how uncomfortable the French Commissioner appeared alongside our men! He had a very high stiff white collar, bow tie, blue serge jacket, drab khaki trousers, and thin button boots! He had already confided to David that he admired his 'équipment', so we imagine he is going to try and get more sensibly rigged our during this Gold Coast visit; it must be ghastly for him and his assistants on travelling days dressed like that.

We pushed off about 8.30, and I walked the first 2 hours—and then hammocked; it was only a 13 odd mile journey to Chira, a good well-kept Ashanti village with a not too bad but old fashioned type of rest-house. The way there was dull, mostly cocoa farms, which in practice 'by road' means paths between bushes some 14 feet high—monotonous and infinitely boring at any time. There was one pleasant thing about it—the telegraph wire was a companion all the way, for it took that line from Sunyani to Nkoranza, and then turned South-east to Coomassie and the world!

Ross had asked us to arrange for a new rest-house at Chira although it was not in our own district, so in the evening with the village elders we settled on a clearing at the side of the forest on a slight rise. Those with us were a philosophic lot, they knew a job had to be done, and that they would have to do it, but even if looking slightly worried, 'Why not agree?' and they do—nodding their heads, and saying something that looks or sounds like 'Oh! yey!' with resigned affiirmation. They may not know it, but they looked so attractive this evening, and dusky with their shoulders bared of their cloths in the brief sunset light at the foot of the vast smooth stemmed cotton trees which are so lofty and brittle looking. The light was a pinky one rapidly dying out to the accompaniment of crickets and other insects starting to tune up for the nightly orchestra.

The follwoing day comes our small boy very early to waken

us saying, 'Ka Kwana lafia' which is the Hausa speech for 'How is your sleep?' to which we make reply 'Lafia lau'. It was a mighty good, cool morning and we set forth at a quarter past six of the clock to march to Nkwansia, a hamlet 22 miles from Chira where we lay the night. (I don't think I can keep up this Pepysian diary style any further). I was very comfortable in breeches, boots and old shirt, and walked for $3\frac{1}{4}$ hours, equivalent to a 10 or 11 mile walk, and David did another hour's walking after that. The road was new at first and the telegraph wire accompanied us most of the way. Alongside somewhere in the bush meandered the old track to Sunyani, and we joined it for about an hour's walking as the road is in the making still. We crossed the Sunyani-Wenchi boundary about 8 o'clock, so we were notified by a board on a tree. David's step grew lighter on finding his foot on his own soil! Further on men and boys were working on the new road. It was funny to look ahead and see the road, rather soft still with one shining, winding, hard track in the middle where people walk. When I say in the middle I am wrong, for that gives the impression of a dead straight line; on the contrary it is similar to the track of an utterly drunk snake! Nevertheless I find that when I am walking I am nearly always mesmerized into following its curvings. I saw some brilliant butterflies but, except for these frail beauties, it is extraordinary how little animal life one sees trekking, all excepting the lines of jet black driver ants pursuing their relentless course across the road, and mysterious birds who unlike good little girls are heard and not seen!

When I got into my hammock I read "Alone in West Africa' by Mary Gaunt, a daring female who adventured herself hither 5 years ago. It is far more interesting to read a book of this sort when one has seen the country oneself. We kept on crossing rivers today, or it may have been the same small river as rivers here seem to pursue as devious a course as the native on the road. I had fun crossing once. I got on to a dead tree and got stuck in the middle as it didn't reach to the other side. One of the Moshi carriers came to the rescue. We could often jump what amounted to a wide ditch but over another bit we tried to cross on a fallen log. The usual method of bridge making is to cut down 2 or 3 handy trees and throw them across. David said he couldn't do what amounted to tight rope walking and after much fumbling of black paws was carried across on a four handed seat while I jeered on the opposite bank. Then it rained, and we hammocked and got our underneaths very wet as the rain dripped down inside the hammocks. Grey skies, thick white mist, squelching bare feet, mud, and sagging garments accompanied us to a little collection of huts where the advanced domestic staff party had been told to go on to and prepare lunch. How different are my experiences to poor Mary Gaunt's who, not knowing the country, language or people, was continually finding her carriers, sitting down, having 'chop' or wanting water, or saying they 'no be fit'.

The rain stopped, we disembarked, sat on chairs under a thatched roof and had Bovril, curry and camp pie. On again at 2 o'clock to Nkwansia, quite a short way, and met by a crowd of villagers who cruised alongside, making music with a bugle, drums and other instruments, shooting past each other, long brown legs flashing, perspiration running off in streams and Manchester cloths on the verge of collapse, held up by good luck and a careless hand. In this wise we cantered up to the rest-house where we tumbled out and David addressed a few 'well chosen' words to the accompanying crowd, thereafter going to see the cattle kraal and other public works while I awaited pots of water for a much needed bath. Later as it was Sunday we had 'church' sitting outside in lovely golden sunset light only spoilt by the devouring sand flies who drove us indoors to put on coats and mosquito boots as we felt quite frantic. Early bed is our lot and our choice. Mama came and announced 'Na gamma' (I have finished [work]) and then adds 'Allah Ya teka gobe' (May God give you tomorrow) or 'Allah Ye tesha mu lafia' (May God raise us up in health) to which we solemnly reply 'Ami', otherwise, 'Amen'.

We have only 5 miles to go to Wenchi our H.Q. today so left quite late at 7.15 a.m. About half way 3 men came up puffing like grampuses, saying that one of the carriers had stolen the Nkwansia chief's stool which he had lent for the kitchen at the rest-house. The story appeared true so David called a halt, bade the 3 men hide in the bush, and we sat down on the roadside on our folding chairs to await the carriers who hove into sight in about 10 minutes. Sure enough the stool was on top of one load so the man was stopped, the Nkwansia-ites emerged from ambush, and a court of enquiry held. The carrier was quite innocent as Mama had told him to take the stool along with him. Consequently the seat was restored, the carrier went on with a guiltless conscience and we proceeded to Wenchi whither Mama had preceded us on his bicycle. The old and new corporals of police and Ansah the town clerk met us. 'Good morning Sah', 'Welcome Missis'. We went on to the town, David enquiring about the work done in his absence. When it came to Ansah saying he had arrested one donkey and a sheep for trespassing on the court and bungalow grounds, I could not help laughing. Dense volumes of smoke rolled across the road where clearing the ground was going on for the building of the new Ashanti town. We were quite glad to get back to our own homestead which appeared intact and the garden in good order. We looked at the distant forest and far away hills beyond which we had travelled in the last fortnight—probably a 200 mile round. Then to come down to more mundane matters David had to question Mama as to his extraordinary behaviour in appropriating the Nkwansia chief's stool, but he was quite frank about it and apparently never thought of stealing but only remembered that he needed a chair for the kitchen at Wenchi and took the first one that came handy! A rather questionable reason! However, all's well that ends well so he was admonished and dismissed!

Then as at home, we got busy round our property, much of the stuff like books, shoes and furnishings having got covered with fungus-like, green mould which is easily wiped off in its early formation. Clipping the Barbadoes pride and bouganvillia and setting fire to fly-breeding cut grass and rubbish finished off a busy day. A lovely evening and sunset over what our predecessor who loved the dense Ashanti forest, called 'those awful Banda hills', followed, which we watched from the verandah steps. David is interviewing the two coporals while I am writing this, for Alamadu the old one returns to Coomassie tomorrow, and Ahmedu takes his place here.

These last days of September have seen David galvanized by the Sunyani visit to awe-inspiring activity in further improvements here. Out betimes with the Clerk striking terror into the hearts of the inhabitants, condemning waste and dirty places, levying fines for ditto and in visions seeing Wenchi as a kind of Utopian garden city with stone-lined and cemented drains for carrying off water, burning ghats for rubbish, and avenues of beautifully grown trees. He often arrived late for lunch having had a long morning in the office and in one case having managed to put the head butcher in prison, for which he was thankful as he is a bad man and a bad influence in the town, but up to date had never been caught out. He is to be tried tomorrow for stealing the sticks with which the hammock boys had marked out their new houses in the town. Moussa (our police orderly) told David that Siberi, who is a rich and important Wangara, was so annoyed last year when he heard David was coming back to Wenchi for a second time, that he went to a Mallam and asked how he could prevent such a catastrophe. The Mallam told him that burying a cow would probably be efficacious as denoting the same fate would overtake David, so he did. He must have been very much annoyed when he found he had buried a cow for nothing! Siberi's friends came to bail him out, but the Court thought a night in prison would cool his head and heels; it is very hard to get witnesses against such a wealthy and influential gentleman, so after the case has been heard tomorrow he will probably have to be allowed to go. As a relief from official problems we went off later with Moussa, Chimsi, and the overjoyed dog to look for 'fakkara' but didn't see or put up any. Moussa says they 'go make eggs' now, and it probably is the close season.

# CHAPTER IV

# Ramadan Ends in 'Salla'

Sunday, October 1st.

We were up betimes and eating our good Scots porridge and eggs at 7.0 prior to walking to Ekrobi, a village about 2 miles away on the Sikassiko road. It is where my husband had Jerichoized the walls of a house which lay across the main road where we passed on a recent trek. We started by way of the Wenchi market where we picked up Osman the Clerk of the Court (whose other names are Edmund Douglas!), and he today was the 'dernier cri' in a black plush Homburg hat, bow tie, tweed jacket, khaki shorts, golf stockings and American laced shoes: An inspection of drains followed in the company of one of the town cleaners who rejoices in the name of Mazzini-bomba. From there, with Moussa our orderly also joining us, we moved off along the Ekrobi track where near the village I spotted a roughly made wooden doll clad in a white garment sitting in an intelligent attitude at the foot of a tree. Thirsting for information I demanded whence came this apparition, but all that Moussa and Osman would say was something about 'medicine' or 'fetish', but no real explanation. Probably some dusky Hannah desiring a son, and following this method of propitiating the Gods—I wonder?

At the village the male population rose up and flocked to meet us, for this small community had lost all (or most of) their houses in a big fire last dry weather, and it was now time to plan for a new one. We were guided to the selected area parallel to the main road, where one of the elders expounded with much gesticulation their ideas to Osman, with the rest standing around like solemn black monkeys in gay printed cloths supported by smaller monkeys in no clothes except a bit of string round their middles. David as solemnly produced a compass which is 'very big medicine' indeed, and amid an awed hush took the bearing of the street; it ran just about N.N.W., but for all it mattered, it might have been due S.W.! While this went on, Hankuri was yelping around chivying she-goats and sheep but no one took an interest in that.

The chief spokesman of the village, Prince Kwesi Bedu, was a very intelligent fellow who had himself planned out the village on his own, and even fixed the measurements for one house to be adopted as a standard size for the village. David, naturally very interested in this, sent Osman and Moussa off with a measuring tape to measure it, and found it was 40 × 40 feet, exactly the size Bedu had estimated and laid out by himself! This was speedily complimented by the Commissioner, who told the Prince that he had 'plenty sense', that building could begin at once, that a prize of £2 would be given for the best built, neatest, and cleanest house, and that we should return in a week or two and see what progress had been made. The business-like attitude of the Chief was most refreshing, as the people are not generally so jolly keen or enterprising where hard work is concerned, and the visit terminated with beaming happiness on both sides. We made for home as quickly as the heat (it was teriffic today) would let us, and arrived dripping but ready for baths, cool clothes, reading, and the Sunday's 'Groundnut', and postprandial siesta; and in the evening a little private Service.

Two or three days later the Zongo chief who had originally brought us pigeons arrived at breakfast time with another 'dash' for me, and when I was called to the door a girl came forward with an enamelled basin on her head with six fine big yams in it, while a paunchy little boy clothed simply in smiles followed with a fat white hen under his arm; the old gentleman looking like one of the patriachs received my thanks very grace-fully. It turned out that this gift was a seasonal one, as the Mahommedan New Year's Day is only three days away—and everyone gives presents then, and also has at least one day's whole holiday. On the same evening as my Zongo friend's 'dash', we ourselves were coming back from an inspection of the three more important Zongos when on looking up the hill we saw a splendid sight.

About 200 head of cattle coming slowly down the red road, or dotted about on the green grass verges, and headed by a crowd of blue and white robed drovers, butchers, and brokers with two horsemen leading them. We waited by the side of the road to see them pass, and David got hold of the chief Wenchi cattle broker, and talked to him in Hausa about the journey, the numbers, and the time it had taken to reach our part of the world. It seems that there were over 200 head, all having come from French Senegal and the Niger some 400 miles away, and with two (seems rather understated?) only lost, they being swept away by a flood crossing the Volta, which is the only really big river between us and the Niger itself. The bulls were fine, great long-horned humped creatures with placid faces, and the whole thing merged into a gorgeous evening picture on which the pale half moon beamed from a wonderfully clear blue sky.

Sunday, October 8th turned out to be the great day, the 'salla' and the feast which is dependent on the tenth day of the new moon, and eagerly watched for by the Mahommedan communities. David and I gave the police a present of a sheep, all the servants having a holiday and turning out in their best clothes to visit the mosques, greet their friends, and share in festivities. We ourselves were prepared to be rather on our own, having seen Moussa, Mama, and Bawi going off to the mosque all clad in flowing robes, but during the morning we heard a drum-tapping getting nearer and nearer which obviously denoted someone of importance coming to greet us, and so it was.

Across the compound came a procession headed by much be-hatted and be-robed Hausas beating drums. In the middle rode old Mallam Azu, the chief of the Hausa Zongo, aged about 70 who had actually as it were founded the Wenchi Zongo 50 years ago by planting a big tree which is there today in the marketplace. We went out to photograph them in the compound, which D. explained was a very lucky thing to have done on a New Year's Day and brings good all the year. The men were nearly all dark and solemn looking, swathed in white and blue robes topped by large straw hats on the wrappings, and carrying spears or staves, with leather charms hung about their persons; a few women in the background, and a lot of little boys with heads shaved except for a bit about a 5/- piece size in front. Them Mallam Azu dismounted showing gorgeous display of coloured embroidered trouser-leg, and came up to shake hands with us, uttering many pious sentiments and wishes—a great deal about 'Allah' and 'M'A'dillah, Allah'*— the elders round about echoing his exclamations. He said how he had been at the mosque praying since daylight, and had come up to salute us before we tasted food. Then he mounted and the cavalcade moved off again being drummed across the field down to the village.

It is funny for us to see everyone in their best clothes, as for example, dear old Ali our cook in a pair of white cotton trousers covered by a white Hausa robe made of an old white silk dinner dress given him by Mrs. Ouchterlony (a Sapper's wife at Coomassie), or Moussa in a white robe underneath a dark blue one with blue and white check cotton trousers showing beneath the robes, and brightly coloured leather boots with a pattern worked on them, or his wife Asetu with the policemens' wives who came to salute me in clean clothes, necklaces, umbrellas, and gay handkerchiefs on their heads but alas; black stockings and laced black European shoes! All this one way and another filled our morning, but the afternoon suddenly produced the worst and most severe rainstorm that anyone had ever seen here; the whole house was flooded, the garden like a lake, and the wind and noise made it impossible to speak. As always the storm passed, and we got out for a walk in the evening, had our own little Sunday service and bathed before supper, after which I tackled Claridge's History of the Gold Coast and Ashanti.

No wonder that today, the second day of the feast, seemed a bit more lethargic in the village than usual, as yesterday permission having been given for the slaughtering of meat anywhere instead of the slaughterhouse (and therefore *no* fees), a total of 46 cattle and 150 sheep was reported to David when we visited the various Zongos during the afternoon. There were few of the men about—the holiday is two whole days, and although of course the Ashantis are not concerned with it from a religious point of view, they take the chance of less business which decreases the market and other jobs. Most of the people from the Zongos who appeared today were women, especially small girls all of whom had dances and games for themselves—very picturesque in smart clothes and kerchiefs with the smaller ones leaping about and singing a chorus to time. No Court for three days, and then we ourselves are giving a general 'at home' to everyone as a mark of our appreciation of their reception of us on our arrival here 6 weeks ago.

Wednesday, October 11th.

The party began by Moussa being sent down to the market yesterday with the large sum of £2 10s. put up by ourselves and our staff to purchase the specialities which would be regarded as refreshments by the local guests. The invitations were for 3.0 p.m. in the large rest-house compound, which had to be arranged accordingly during the morning. The result of Moussa's shopping was as follows. Big balls of 'fura' made of millet and pepper, and I don't know what else, which when mixed with water and piled in large enamelled basins makes an apparently savoury and palatable dish; several bottles of eucalyptus, much esteemed as a perfume; tins of Three Castle cigarettes, and quantities of Kola nuts. With all this and more we purposed to feed our guests who in the intervals of not eating Kola and 'fura', and not smoking cigarettes nor drenching themselves with scent, will dance and sing.

After our own luncheon, we changed into our 'braws', and with the police and the prisoners superintended the laying out of chairs, tables, and flags at the welcoming point in the rest-house compound. Our two chairs were put in front of the house between a French and an English flag (Monsieur Prouteaux, the Ivory Coast Commissioner, should have been here if he had not been recalled to Bontuku) and little tables arranged some way off with abundance of Kola nuts, scent, cigarettes, matches, 'fura' and 'water' in big bowls in readiness thereon. About 2,500 people were expected. David said that the result would be a beautifully beaten down compound, and obviate the necessity of clearing it again for some time. The Omanhin lent us a large red State umbrella which was placed between our chairs. About 3.0 p.m. the Corporal came to report that a great many people had already arrived, so in the radiant sunshine we had hoped for we walked up through a large throng to the welcoming point, where the Ashanti king and his suite, the Hausas, Moshis, Wangaras, and Jiminis in groups, were collecting in a semi-circle; it really and truly was a most wonderful sight, and quite took my breath away.

About six of the more important men were mounted on horseback looking barbarically Eastern in appearance; they were clad in red and white turbans and long green embroidered coats, with blue and white robes, with highly peaked decorated saddles and trappings, numerous leather ornaments hanging around the horses bridles and headstalls. One man with a dark saturnine face wore a red and white turban wound all round his head, a long green velvet coat embroidered with yellow, and light yellow riding boots embroidered in a pattern of red, blue, and green. He was really superb, and though the horses are small, dark, weedy specimens yet the riders are wonderful horsemen, and they made their steeds curvet and prance, and buck and jump for showing off; one man had a great trick of making his horse go down on his knees and bow his head like a circus horse. He did this several times in front of us shouting out 'Sanu Zaki' (a term denoting king or chief though its real Hausa terminology is 'lion'). Apart from these doings the way these men gaily rode their horses all over the place regardless of the crowd was astonishing and quite alarming, but apparently nothing happened.

The modern men such as the carpenter and others rode their bicycles round the crowd, and the mixture of civilisation and barbarism was complete; but Wenchi is unique in that respect for the Northern tribes and the Ashanti mingle in it, and it is neither primitive nor yet sophisticated but a kind of half-way house between the Gold Coast proper and the Northern and Central African tribes and peoples.

It was a very hot and noisy party but unparalleled for sightseeing, and the crowd marvellously well-behaved and goodtempered. The six police including Moussa (who had been permitted to get himself up in his Hausa robes) officiated as caterers and presided at the refreshment stalls; soon cigarettes and Kola nuts were being circulated, but I nearly exploded when I saw Moussa going round with a bottle of real Arabian musk scent which he scattered like holy water on the people near him, putting a few drops down this man's neck and again a few drops on that fair lady's face or hands. Added to that he wore one chammy-leather glove (where he had got it from, Lord knows) and a wrist watch on his right hand. The rest of his costume consisted of white and blue striped very full trousers covered by a long white slip-over garment, a small white cap rather like the old-fashioned clown's peaked felt hat, red and yellow socks, and gaily coloured leather boots of native make. A little later I saw him gyrating solemnly in the group directly in front of us which was a dancing party of Moshi men.

Their dance was quite one of the most interesting I've seen, just like an old English Morris dance. The men dance in a big circle each armed with a short stick, and they tap it against their neighbour's, twist round and tap it against their neighbour's on the opposite side, and go right round in that wise. In the middle 2 or 3 men play kettle-drums with their hands. The costumes were too varied and wonderful to describe, and the graceful twirls and spirit they put into the dance was extraordinary while their energy was untiring and their time perfect. They have a wonderful ear for rhythm and time these people.

Beyond them the Wangaras were dancing, men and women armed with horsetails which they wave slowly, and go through a lot of slow shuffling movements with their feet and arms.

The Jiminis' delightful orchestra was playing on our left surrounded by a semi-circle of their people; anyone who stepped out executed a 'pas seul' as they felt inclined. One girl danced with a handkerchief, another with an ordinary umbrella which she held in front of her or above her head and contorted her body in slow wriggling movements, doing funny short shuffling steps with her feet. The men danced more energetically leaping in the air, twisting round, throwing their legs about, sinking down to the ground, making faces, and looking madder than any inhabitant of Bedlam.

I didn't know where to look, the colour, the people, the dances, were all so attractive and bewildering. One man had an ordinary English 'Bobby's' helmet on: where on earth he had got it, I don't know. The girls were doing their quaint dance in another circle, clapping their hands, and singing and throwing or rather jumping each other in turns up into the air. Various chiefs came and saluted us besides the trick rider on the horse. The Jiminis advanced at close range, and while their

Chief bowed, several of the orchestra played their instruments almost sitting upon my legs for about 5 minutes: deafening. The Hausas staid and grave and dignified as ever also came up, and the Wangara Chief approached and gave us the benefit of a solo dance almost on our toes, and under our sheltering umbrella, waving a fly-whisk meanwhile. He was so tall that there was only just room for him; he ended up by throwing himself on the ground and bowing before David to the earth, which is a most unusual obeisance for this part of the world. These people often look so fierce when they come closing in to salute one that it looks quite alarming, till you realise that their intentions are eminently peaceful and friendly.

The young girls, and the little ones, were too delicious in bright cloths tied round their waists and gaudy handkerchiefs on their heads, their necks hung round with silver chains and ornaments. I saw three great tall young men in long bright yellow coats worn over white trousers with little white caps, which formed a most effective costume. The Omanhin himself under his personal State umbrella appeared to be enjoying the fun. He was smoking a Three Castle cigarette with great relish, clad in one of those becoming handwoven patchwork Ashanti cloths, with the intelligent Prince Kwasi Bedu sitting beside him —the same who is laying out Ekrobi village with such skill— and a good many of his people.

We stayed for an hour, and watched the fun; it is a great thing to be entertained at one's own garden party! Mama the house boy came and said our tea was ready, so we went back to our own house and rested a bit with books, but returned at a quarter past five to see the people before they left. We moved about 'freely' (I think this is the correct term), and mingled with the crowd, David shaking hands with all the Chiefs and the Omanhin, saying how glad he was to see them. Everyone smiled, looked happy, and showed sets of almost incredibly perfect white teeth. The gay crowd melted away—the Ashanti umbrellas waving and bobbing down the road; by six o'clock not a soul was left and in the village some drums and songs continued until complete silence reigned pretty soon after nine o'clock.

ENTRANCE TO FORT AT COOMASSIE

WENCHI MARKET

WOMEN POUNDING FU-FU

THE OMANHIN OF TEKIMAN

# CHAPTER V

# Local Travelling

After the garden party there was no particular incident either in the town or at the Courthouse which took long to deal with, so David suddenly decided that a few days travel to some villages off the normal track had better be done, and on 18th October without much preparation we took the world for our pillow again. As usual the domestic staff rose to the occasion at short notice with the result that we got steam up and were under way by a quarter to 8. Our camp following was considerably less in number than the Sikassiko tour; it was good walking on the Kintampo road (actually a sandy bush track) so that we soon reached a small village called Akette where there are two elements, Ashanti and North country, as the road from Bole in the N.W. corner of the N.T. comes in here.

At this time of year there is a constant stream of Moshis coming down to Wenchi and Sunyani province for kola nuts. It is all very pretty open country, well watered, with patches of forest. Soon after 11.0 we reached a village called Ngoase, and while Ali was preparing luncheon (spatchcocked bushfowl and a cheese omelette on an open fire with a minimum of cooking utensils!) we inspected the village, and were able to congratulate the people on its good layout and cleanliness; it had a very fine fetish house with two or three big drums lying outside.

Afterwards we hammocked along a path between forest and open land for about two hours going, but no villages. Then just before getting to Nchira where we were to lie the night, the sound of drumming was heard, presently a bobbing umbrella was seen, and most of its population hove in sight, making as the psalmist says, a joyful noise. This proceeded from three enormous bottle-shaped drums carried on men's heads and beaten with little crooked sticks or rather bent ones. A small modern drum contributed its quota to the sounds of jollity, a rather cracked bugle was blown, one or two parchment-covered square wooden things were beaten by hand, and best of all a gin bottle, hit with a small stick, gave out the sound of a cracked chapel bell.

This place is on the Kintampo road, Kintampo itself being only about 24 miles away. Tomorrow we have to turn back on our tracks a little bit, and then strike across to Wufoma only three hours march from here. The best sight of today, I think, was Bawi leaving the lunch camp. He strode off—strode is the only word for his business-like way of walking tho' I don't suppose his tender years number more than ten or eleven summers— his whole being was more glorious than Solomon's. A non-descript pink and dark brown cloth was tied round him and fastened in a knot at the back of his neck, he wore a pair of brilliant green puttees on his ridiculous little brown legs, and his entire head and almost shoulders were hidden by an old policeman's helmet, the same one that we noticed at our garden party. I don't think I ever saw anyone cut such a rum figure! We had tea at 3.30 and David held a palaver afterwards with the chief and his people. After that we were presented with 'dashes'; some yams and a particularly nice, white, sheep fell to my lot.

October 19th. We had a very short trek this morning to Wufoma, only three hours altogether. It was a lovely, sunny morning when we got up at 6 o'clock, rather like a very bright, autumn one at home, sunshine tipping the surrounding bushes and gilding the tree tops. We burnt a small house down before we left that had to be destroyed. The roof was a bit damp, but once the thatch caught it blazed and smoked fiercely and eventually fell in. We were under way about 7 o'clock and I walked for the first hour, but it was a pretty hot day and I hammocked the rest while David walked till within 10 minutes of Wufoma. It was a cleared bush path all the way through open patches of grassland and thick, dense, crowding-in forest; there was actually one really rushing river with waterfalls and boulders which made a pleasant sound like a stream at home.

Wufoma boasts of one of Mr. D. Boyle's superior rest-houses, on which we suddenly burst in a cleared space out of the long grass; after putting down all our belongings, we went off to the village a few yards further on, a regular Ashanti village with cocoa beans, smelling like bad beer, spread out on mats resting on platforms of stakes to dry. Very good hunting country all round here, but grass much too long at present to be of any use. We went up to the fetish house at the top of the long main village street. It was built of thatch the whole way up, a long pointed conical hive, about 25 feet high with a very little opening at the bottom, in fact it was exactly like a bee skep. We wished we could go in, but such policy is hardly advisable as the community might be wrathful. We took a photograph of it anyhow. From there it was no distance to the centre of the village where the chief and his elders were awaiting us under a great spreading ficus tree of some kind. There was a short palaver but they seemed to have no complaints so back to the rest-house, where 'dashes' arrived, also a local mail from Sunyani.

We shall have to remain here tomorrow, as instructions had come for Osman to be despatched at once back to Wenchi to call up all the reservists of the W.A.F.Fs. of which there were a lot in that town. They are being called up to garrison Coomassie while drafts from the headquarters there are being sent out to the army in East Africa. After the midday meal and a rest, we walked down with the women and girls to the river where they were washing clothes, and filling their pots, calabashes and gourds for the return with them poised on their heads, a pleasant domestic picture in the sunset rays. I saw one or two scraggy-necked old hornbills flying overhead, and a 'fakara' was calling in the long grass while crickets shrilled all round. Back in the village street the people were putting away the cocoa beans for the night, they had been baking and drying in the sun all day; many of the population were standing about in the doorways looking at the strange white faces. Very few white men have ever been to this village, probably only Captain Kortright in the 1900 war, a Mr. Fell (D's. previous P.C.), Mr. Wood, and D. himself; while I am the first white woman to set a foot in it. As we passed one group, a diminutive naked brown infant of about 2 years old exclaimed loudly and clearly

59

'Dada' as David went by. I said 'I hope not', and D. turned to the child and said 'Pardon me; I think you've made a mistake' or words to that effect. The onlookers all smiled, though the point of the remark was lost on them, but it really sounded very funny.

Next day (Friday, October 20th) was a rare one for us, no duties of any kind—so we read, wrote letters, and generally lazed until Osman returned about tea time, after which we sent our chairs to the village tree where a palaver was to take place, and followed with Moussa and Osman. The chief and the most important people were already there, with the rest as near as possible all around; Moussa stood behind us, and Osman in front to interpret. It was a quaint scene. The chief with his grizzled beard and brilliant Josephian robe draped round him on his low brass-studded chair, the others solemn, brown and dusky, squatting on low Ashanti stools or on the ground. The evening was very still and fine, and a few brids twittered and chattered in the trees. David first spoke about the new paper money, and the cocoa trade, and then heard any complaints going. They are 'no blate', and the complainers trot to the fore with great 'sang froid' and declaim vigorously. How Osman remembers all they say, and puts it into concise English, I don't know; there is a great deal of pink-palmed dusky hands, and nodding and wagging of heads—it is really most amusing to watch. There was a long case about a stolen fetish, and then an adultery one, another about guns—nothing wildly interesting but all funny to watch and hear. All the dozens of grave solemn faces fixedly gaze on us, our own hammock boys and men also among the crowd. A palaver is a sort of free amusement I suppose. When back at the rest-house a boy aged 16 from the Church of England School at Coomassie got an interview as he wants to be a clerk, and had been sent to us by the Chief of Pulliano. He could talk English quite well. David asked him who we were fighting and, on his reply 'the Germans', asked 'Are they good people?', to which the lad replied 'No, very bad men, Sir'—and when asked who in the Bible had said something about preparing the way, the boy said 'St. John' after only a moment's thought. He is going to accompany us now, and when back at Wenchi can be tried out for a permanent job. (Curse these sandflies! I'm writing out of doors and they attack me continually, with the result that my hands and face are covered with spots).

October 21st. We were called this morning at 5 o'clock, and when I went to look outside the waning moon overhead was still shining brightly, and the Southern Cross showed faintly low down as the dawn came up. It was very beautiful and cool; we dressed by lamplight and all of a sudden it was day. Off we started at about a quarter to six, David taking his rifle as there is game in this area—Moussa came with us and the hammock boys and house boys were bidden to keep well behind us to start with. We were going through an open bite of wood country when suddenly quite a big green and brown snake about 4 feet long dropped out of a tree just in front of us, overhanging the path, and wriggled away among the grass. Hankuri like a silly fool started to go after it but we called him back. Very soon we saw some quite fresh hartebeeste tracks and some smaller ones, probably duiker, but never a startled head or a pair of horns could we see showing among the long succulent grass. I slew two large tsetse flies on David's back, and Moussa killed some on mine as we were walking single file—silent and alert, and we went steadily on till we reached Boyem about 9 o'clock. This extraordinary out of the way village is tucked away in a fertile cuplike hollow at the bottom of an immense hill, with another similar one on the other side. A grand cocoa and kola country just here, and the farms are excellent. It had been a $3\frac{1}{4}$ hour walk when we got down to the village, and the chief and elders had received us; we had planned to lunch there, but being so early we just spent a restful half hour in this happy spot and had drinks out of our thermos flasks while the eight post-to-post carrier loads were dumped down and then sent on by the Boyem people to Tuobodom where we were to spend the night.

Before going on David held a palaver with the chief and his people, discussed cocoa and other matters, while they produced one case for him to adjudicate—one of the eternal 'cherchez la femme' cases which were so common in this country. Meanwhile the belles of the village produced cooked yams in black earthen platters for the hammock boys. The next eleven miles or so took us to Tuobodom, a big village on the Tekiman/Kintampo road, where we had to put up in a native house as there is no rest-house yet. I was rather pleased as it was for the first time, and we got the chief's house, practically two joined together with open red-beaten earth courtyards in the centre and raised open platforms round with white and red pillars, and shingle roofs over the platforms. Our belongings were deposited in various recesses, table and chairs in one, and beds in another—the largest one. This is definitely a regular old fashioned village; I noticed one particularly tall house for Ashanti, some two-storeys high and on its outside wall a rough raised design of a crocodile made of the same white stuff as the walls. Then lunch and a rest, but David had a little court work. We went out later in the afternoon (having with some difficulty managed each to get a bath in the middle of a sudden thunderstorm) and soon passed the fetish house (for that is what the tall one is) on our way across the small river to see where the rest-house will be built. Before our arrival orders had been given for a large area to be cleared; to the village seldom visited before, this is an important innovation. David and Moussa soon got it marked out while I watched the women washing clothes in the river, and noticed that a great many people here seemed to suffer from goitre and guineaworm, perhaps caused by bad water or perhaps by parasites of some sort. We dined in the open centre of the chief's house to the noise of the women beating fu-fu for their meals, the crickets inevitable chorus, and our meal lighted and beautified by God's ceiling with stars beginning to show as night began.

Today, being Sunday October 22nd, and only a short march in front of us, we got up later than usual and had breakfast at 7.0. Then while our kit was being packed and the carriers getting ready, we walked down into the village where, under and round the ubiquitous great tree in the middle, the Chief and the people in general were grouped. On the way we saw another outside wall of the big fetish house with a bas-relief of a leopard, and another of a monkey carrying a sword of state.

The meeting started by the Commissioner blowing the authorities up sky-high, notably a dirty village, refusal to work as the bailiff who had preceded us had ordered, and no chief or linguist representing him to meet us outside the village as is accepted etiquette. For these misdeeds they had been fined after our arrival to the tune of £10, but owing to the quick clearance of the rest-house ground and the absolute city of the dead last night (not a noise to be heard) £6 was remitted to the vulture-like old linguist, in a pocket handkerchief! Apart from this we arrested one young man who had been very insolent and refused to work and had to be made an example for others. The young blood of this part of the District are being very troublesome and resenting the chief's powers. He was got awfully neatly, as Osman spotted him squatting among the crowd and showed him quietly to David. He in turn sent a hammock boy to Moussa who was just seeing off the carriers, and then when Moussa appeared behind the crowd David motioned to him exactly where the young man was, and Moussa dashed in and had him handcuffed at once.

As it was only 6 or 7 miles to Tekiman we both walked all the way being met by a Tekiman sword bearer at the Tano river, after crossing which we had to undergo the usual vocal school-children alternating with Loyal or Moody & Sankey choruses! Arriving at the rest-house David, having arranged to hold court on arrival, left me and went on to his palaver at the court house where the chief was already awaiting him. After a meal and a rest, the Omanhin came round to call on us, and we all walked together into the town, the Zongo, and the Mission garden before sunet. Then sitting outside the rest-house we had our weekly small private service before dinner and beds. Next day it was 15 or 16 miles to Nkwansia, and a very hot day, and after a comparatively short (6 or 7 miles?) walk we both hammocked. At that point the road was wide and level which gave the boys a chance of a race, so before we knew what had happened the two teams were simply flying along, nearly joggling us out of the hammocks like ships at sea, or in my case like riding before you can rise properly in the saddle! In the end we practically finished up level, crushed against the rest-house wall!

Next day (October 24th) we got back to Wenchi quite early —it is only five miles from Nkwansia—and we found everything in good order, the flower beds blooming, the town repairs and new houses all in hand, and a lot of court work awaiting David.

My 25th birthday and the 25th October! I have now completed a quarter of a century's term of life, which is a way of putting it that makes me feel very old indeed. David was scuttling about in his pyjamas at an early hour preparing surprises. Besides the Jack, a French, Russian, Italian, Belgian flag, plus another Union Jack, float from one flagstaff. The office is closed so Osman gets a holiday and only a half day's work in the garden is done by the hammock boys. When breakfast came I sat on a lovely big Ashanti stool which David had made for me by the Nkwansia Chief, and there were two smaller ones as well. The silversmith had been told by David to make me a pair of small silver bracelets, a ring, and a Mahommedan charm—all real native work. Osman, Ali, Mama, and Moussa, all came to salute me and were too sweet. They knew it was my birthday, and all gave me presents. Ali gave me a pair of wonderful Hansa leather slippers and white cowtail fly-whisk, Mama an ostrich feather whisk, Moussa 15 eggs, and Osman a whip.

Nay more! Osman's wife's sister, Abina, and two boys came up with two pawpaws, a dish of rice, a beautifully carved calabash filled with groundnuts, a large bunch of bananas, besides some eggs. Eggs! Eggs! The sky fairly rained them down, for the butcher Alberi had also heard of this auspicious occasion somehow, and sent a large dish of guinea-fowl eggs, and the Wangaras sent a fowl, yams, and more eggs. How on earth we are going to eat them all I don't know! I see visions of eggs poached, eggs fried, eggs buttered, eggs scrambled, eggs omeletted, eggs boiled, and son on down a long mysterious and monotonous vista. We should have an election here—then the less fresh ones would come in really useful!

In the afternoon, which was a very hot one, old Mallam Azu came full of bows and genuflections bringing fowls, eggs and yams as a present for me. He took my hand in his withered brown ones and shook it gently, and then touched his breast and forehead and murmured all kinds of pious ejaculations and wishes. I like the old man; he has been to Mecca in his younger days and is a fine ancient, and a rare old Mahommedan. We had intended to go out to some of the farms after tea and look out for a partridge ('fakara') or bustard, but with a really bad storm brewing on the south side we gave that up and organised a game of football for the boys and the police on the rest-house ground, with some jumping practice nearer our own house. The lightning flashed all over the place but, except for some ten minutes fierce rain, the storm gave us a miss and blew on to the Banda hills near Menge and the N. Territories. To end the day, a very superior dinner completed my 25th birthday, the first married one and the first in a 'far country'; I doubt if I'll ever again have such a quaint and original one.

*MENU*
Turtle Soup
Prawn Cake
Roast Mutton
Asparagus
Plum Pudding
Dessert — Brandy Peaches
Coffee

The following day we received a home mail which should have reached us on the 25th.—The first letter I opened was from my father telling me of three family deaths, Mark Tennant on September 20th, Bim my dearest cousin on 22nd, Raymond Asquith on 18th—all within a week. At such moments for us, left behind, life seems to stand still, there is neither past nor future only a kind of suspended stricken present. But we must go on, and be brave and happy, for that is what they would tell us to be if they could speak. Only it is almost harder to go on living than to die as they did.

After finishing the monthly accounts, Osman and all of us (including the Commissioner) seemed to have had rather a slack time, so we decided that we would have a rest inside as well as out, and would go twenty-four hours without food as an experiment in health service. The test began on October 31st by having breakfast at 8.30 a.m. (David eating 5 boiled eggs— they are small out here) and after that nothing until breakfast at the same time on November 1st, except a cup of tea (one only) at 4.0 p.m., and a bar of plain chocolate. We both felt rather odd when the times for luncheon and dinner came round, but bore up all right. The only real difficulty was the explaining to the servants when they came as usual after breakfast for orders. David said 'No lunch' and 'No dinner' and Ali looked quite upset, while in the background Mama laughed as he thought it was a good joke; but brilliantly inspired, David explained it was a 'salla' or fast day—one of the only ways of explaining the apparent madness to a Mahommedan. May he be forgiven!, though there is Hallowe'en to counter it. Later on I saw Mama wearing a little white Hansa robe over his trousers, and discovered that this was an act of courtesy to a 'salla'. Some four days later David went down with a dose of fever, from which this tour he had so far not suffered, and retired to bed. This makes it difficult for us to do a proposed tour in the Jaman district in order to number the Dane guns—an exercise which has to be done yearly—so Osman and Moussa will have to be sent on bicycles round the villages to tell the people they must bring their guns in here.

It was November 7th before this annoying bout of fever left David and he is still a bit off colour but, although he had to do a certain amount of office work up here in the house, he is lucky only to be that after the events of last night. The people in the village were making a tremendous row about 9 o'clock, talking and yelling at the pitch of their voices, and a little later when I was just going to bed David took it into his head to go down and see the policeman guarding the Court (for money is kept there) and incidentally ask him 'why the? and what the?' didn't he go and stop the town row. It was bright moonlight, so David suggested that I should put his Burberry on over my select slumberwear and accompany him. All was still as the grave now, and the clear moon showed up the pattern of the fern-like flamboyant trees on the avenue, while I waited at a discreet distance watching David disappear into the shadow of the courthouse. No noise came, and no one was to be seen till he threw a stone on to the roof, when a husky voice challenged him and Abdul Dagomba appeared from under the Court table inside, where after further investigation his sweetheart was also discovered. David shouted to me then to go home as he would have to go round the the Clerk's house with the policeman and his ladylove, and have him charged with neglect of duty and whatnot. So I wandered back home again. This morning the case had to be disposed of early in order to let Osman and Moussa start off to Jaman before it became too hot for bicycling; we for the first time are now left rather on our own here without Clerk or Orderly, and rather short of police too with one in prison instead of guarding us! Luckily the young Christian Clerk we took on at Wufoma is now acting as the Omanhin's clerk here, and was called in to help me copy some letters at the Court, David lying up again with a bad headache after his last night's adventure.

Next day was uneventful, but the invalid and I managed a quiet walk in the cool of the evening, inspected the Zongos and on return to the house were treated to a remarkable sight—the full pale moon and the round red sun with wisps of cloud drifting across the face of each in a direct line opposite one another. 'The moon on my right hand, the sun on my left'—the song exactly, most unusual and beautiful. Keeping an eye on things ourselves we took the Corporal Ahmedu and did a tour of the village on the following morning, David taking his gun to shoot some of the kites there which were always swooping down on small chickens—as a result we were soon followed by a crowd of young people cheering the successful shots and dashing in to pick up spent cartridge cases. All seemed going on as usual, but we soon had a surprise before lunch in the shape of the arrival on bicycle of 'white man come' as announced by Mama. It was a little party of three Wesleyan Mission Members who were making a tour of our part of Ashanti, and of whom we had been warned but not given date of arrival. My first thought was how to turn lunch for two in lunch for five, three of whom will obviously be really hungry! But as ever the native domestic staff rose to the occasion as their Asiatic opposite numbers do, or their Irish prototypes for that matter. Having first directed our guests to the rest-house for a wash and brush up we were at table not much later than usual, with a meal consisting of a large stew, including bacon, kidneys, mushrooms and macaroni, fresh corn with butter, and tinned plums, sardines, and other accessories (Fortnum & Mason had a good deal to do with it, as usual!). Two of our guests were young, a Mr. Roe and a Mr. Armstrong, but the third, by name Maude, was a fine sporting old fellow aged about 70 years; he had made twenty-one double voyages to and from England and first landed in Africa approximately 50 years ago, before Wolseley and the modern coast history.

Our guests were not only a very nice surprise but were themselves most interesting on the tribal and general African mode of life, for they saw sides of it which we did not see, and found difficulties and problems which we had not got to cope with. In the cool of the evening we got the two younger ones to play tennis with us but as they had no racquets we perforce only played singles—and all four thus managed to get some good games. Next morning we took them at 8.30 in the cool of the day to make a grand tour of our village, all the Zongos, and the market, and the encampment where donkeys were loading up with kola nuts. The Jiminis earned good marks from our guests, which pleased us, as they are a fine lot of people, hard-working, and give no trouble; most of them are immigrants from French country, like the Segus of whom there have been quite a large inrush recently—an odd lot who wear their hair rather like fetish men in funny little plaits round their heads. Mr. Maude said that quite often they had saluted him with 'Bon Jour, Monsieur' on the road up from Coomassie.

David was terribly pleased when Mr. Maude told him that Wenchi was the best laid out African town that he had ever seen, a genuine tribute from a man who had first landed in West Africa in 1867, while I glowed with wifely pride! Two days later our Missionary friends left on their bicycles for Kintampo, Mr. Maude as fit and active as his young companions; their carriers start earlier, so we gave the bicyclists a good breakfast and saw them off at 8.30. Today in the afternoon Osman and Moussa returned from Sampa (the local name for Sikassiko), having completed the gun tour as ordered. The other day a former hammock boy named Lasanna turned up from far away North in the Moshi country; apparently he had heard that David was back at Wenchi again, and was determined to return and work for him another tour—which although it was not easy to arrange for lack of funds has been arranged, and he is now very happy working in the garden. As in India those who work for their white rulers cling to the jobs, and frequently return after being paid off months before.

The day I am writing has been remarkable for excessive rain and wind so much so that we were, at least in the morning, rather marooned in the house; anyhow we didn't waste our time as we played chess, piquet and patience, and I had a Hansa lesson from David, a Gaelic one to myself, and then tried him with a German one. After luncheon we went down to the Court, where we saw stacks of the Dane guns which have been brought in for registration, great long single barrel things bought in Birmingham for about 5/- and sold at Coomassie for about 25/-. They are hand loaded with powder and hold masses of nails and slugs—pretty sure to kill anything dead at 50 yards or so, but the African bush sportsman is not only a good stalker but also a fairly good shot, so the ownership of a Dane gun is a useful method of getting 'meat' in its widest sense. The next morning there seemed to be hundreds of the Jaman people about, for it was their area and their villages which had brought the guns in for registration, so that during the cataloguing and stamping of the guns at the Court, their owners were able to improve the Commissioner's garden and clear the vicinity of all bush and long grass, dangerous in the dry weather when fires spread like rivers in spate unless some defensive gaps of this kind can be made in and around farms and villages. Our temporary gardeners and conscripted workers treated this as an exciting interlude, for from time to time there were yells and shrieks of delight when they came upon a rodent of sorts, whereupon they all pursued the luckless animal and killed it, but the killing is not prompted by sport for this animal is regarded as a delicacy—I was shown one like a cross between a large rat and an otter, with stiff and short bushy hair. One lot of workers came across, and killed, a very large puff-adder—about 3½ feet long, with a wicked head. This also was brought to me for inspection, while a little crowd gathered round, including Moussa's two wives and Tani and Asetu who squealed and giggled just like domestics at home when the garden boy showed them a worm, or if they themselves see a mouse. David got another dose of fever today and had to retire to bed again.

It is now November 23rd, and there has been practically nothing to write about for the last four or five days. All the guns were eventually stamped and had been returned with their owners to the Jaman country—over 1,000 was the final total. All the building in the town is going well—there have been no political or criminal disturbances, and we have had no home mail so were glad to get news from Bontuku. This told us that both our hosts there, M. Prouteaux and his assistant M. Chaumel, were going shortly, the young one to another post in the Ivory Coast and M. Prouteaux to France on leave after five years without seeing his own country. Our set-up here has been changed as regards the police, for David found that we required more and tougher men now that the town has grown so rapidly; the midnight Court breach of duty showed up the lack of discipline which was beginning to have effect. Gale, the head of the Police in Coomassie responded at once, and only yesterday a sergeant of some standing and five stalwart constables arrived to take over the post here. Today when we ourselves are on the point of retiring to Menge, a quiet village on the Jaman road, for a few day's complete change and rest, we took the new sergeant round the Zongos and the Ashanti village—and introduced him to Osman the clerk, who will be keeping an eye on everything during our sort of week-end off! It was pleasant in the town, with lots of donkeys arriving from the North to get loaded up with kola nuts, and no small numbers of cattle drovers there also on the way down to the Coast. We are travelling very light, one hammock and very few of the servants, no clerk, and only Moussa with one rather amusing new policeman, a Yoruba called Bodamassie who had been a soldier in the Cameroon show, and now has joined the police. It was rather sad parting with our nice little Corporal Ahmedu, but David assured him it was not his fault that the changes had to be made; a good report as to his work here went with him to Mr. Gale personally. I am writing this in an improvised camp on the bank of the Tain river, where we arrived this afternoon on the first (only 7 miles) stage of the road to Menge and Bontuku.

# CHAPTER VI

# Christmas at Wenchi

At Menge. Sunday November 26th. We are completing our little weekend holiday tomorrow, and are already all the better for the change. Not only have we been away from people and houses, and even noises at times, but we had the luck to choose this perfect little sanctuary which lies among quite high hills, two of them rather resembling the Paps of Jura, though probably only about half that height.—It was appropriate therefore that we should have a real home Sunday morning, late breakfast (with sausages!), our own little service with 'I to the hills will lift mine eyes', and a feeling that we were nearer a kindred atmosphere. After the usual hot afternoon we even did a little bit of hill climbing, accompanied by 3 or 4 of the hammock boys who thought it great fun. As we made for home a troop of monkeys crossed the path in front of us, which delighted my soul. They were a little bigger than the barrel organ variety. I shouted my pleasure, and found an 'echo' so 'the mountains' shouted for joy, and the hills clapped their hands.

December 2nd.—A new month is now in progress. I saw yesterday in the cattle market (we arrived back at Wenchi 4 days ago) a lot of pure white birds like seagulls and found out that they were a kind of egret called here 'cowbirds' which travel down from the North with the cattle, and perch on the animal's backs probably deriving subsistence of some sort from the hides —quite a new thing to see here. Today we were making ready to go to Tekiman where we have been summoned to meet the Chief Commissioner and his wife (Mr. and Mrs. Fuller) who are touring Ashanti on his annual inspection, and luckily had arranged only to leave this afternoon and stay at Nkwansia

(5 miles out) and then tomorrow straight on the other 16 miles to Tekiman. While at breakfast a white sergeant of the W.A.F.F. appeared on his way to Kintampo to recruit for the regiment. He had come from Sunyani, and travelled in the early dawn so as to rest during the day, it being especially hot just now. We were glad to give him welcome, and a jolly good breakfast. Name of Jones, and a colour sergeant of the good old type, hard bitten and keen. In his time he had been in China, S. Africa, Ireland, the West Indies, fought and wounded at Mons in the 1914 retreat, and then served in the Cameroons. He was delightfully outspoken, but looked rather seedy as poor fellow he had been suffering from boils while at Sunyani, and now to suffer from a different set of 'boyles' seemed too much of a good thing! He was remarkably good company but rather depressed though talked away cheerfully to D. while I was silently survey-ing with undisguised interest his heavily tattooed arms! A Geisha girl, another lass of British persuasion, two clasped hands, a flying bird, the name 'Albert', and a few other 'objets d'art'.

David took him away to the rest-house after breakfast, and I was able to arrange a good luncheon with us before we our-selves had to leave. To this meal after a rest he returned much more cheerful, and we had a grand talk, mainly on military subjects, and the present War. He was rather nice about the Dardanelles as for example 'I'm not a brave man, and not a coward, but God Almighty I'd have thought twice before volun-teering for *that* palaver', and went on to say 'Sir Ion (*his* pronunciation) Hamilton's tactics were as withered as his arm!' —His candour was most refreshing. There is no beating about the bush with these people. David said something about wanting to take a part in the War, whereupon he said 'Don't you worry. You'd be no use there!'—We gave him lots of books and papers, then departing ourselves at 2.0 p.m. in the great heat meeting the mail on the road, so were able to open it, read a bit in our hammocks, and then subside in the rest-house for a quiet evening, and a good sleep (we hope) before our 16 miles journey tomorrow.

Sunday December 3rd finds us at Tekiman, nearing which as always we had to endure the usual heartrendering and penetrating chorus of the school children. The good Omanhin greeted us at the rest-house where he was superintending the

THE MOSQUE AT WENCHI

CHRISTIANSBORG CASTLE-ENTRANCE, WITH H. S. NEWLANDS, SIR HUGH CLIFFORD'S
PRIVATE SECRETARY

BONTUKU, WITH FRENCH COMMISSIONER

DAVID BOYLE AND ORDERLY WITH SERGEANT

clearance of bush all around, exhorting and commanding for an hour or so.

As we were leaving the new rest-house for the Chief Commissioner's occupation, we were compelled to return to the old Ashanti-type one which is the regular quadrangle building but in bad condition with an open courtyard in the middle, this can be quite comfortable unless a really big storm blew up; Alas! that is what did happen, and we were hardly asleep when in less than 10 minutes our beds were getting wet, Mama had to be called, and both of us with him strove to move all our beds, mosquito curtains, etc. into another alcove sheltered from the driving gale. Luckily we had dined, and had our little Sunday service, and were bathed before dark—but it was a ghastly night, and Monday morning didn't find us keen to rise as early as usual. The Fullers had been expected to arrive before midday, but a message came that they would be later in the day, so we, and the Omanhin and his people, had time to clean up the two resthouses, and also the main parts of the little town and put all in the good order. These big storms do a lot of damage to thatched houses, and this one nearly broke up two of the old resthouse walls, which had not made our night any happier!

At about 2.30 Moussa who had been reconnoitering on his bicycle arrived to say that the great ones were arriving, so David moved off in his hammock to meet them in the town. Dane guns were being fired, horns and drums going strong, and the children chorusing, while I watched the sight from the round house; it was quite amusing. First came numerous small boys carrying Ashanti chairs on their heads, then the Omanhin dressed in his best and sitting in a wicker litter carried on men's heads under a large red umbrella. He looked most imposing sitting up there with a kind of sceptre in his hand, and a 'Pickelhaube' on his head, preening himself. Then more dusky hosts in their hammocks followed by the Zongo people—in fact it seemed like the whole Tekiman population. I emerged, and we shook hands. Mrs. Fuller is the last white woman I spoke to, and that was 4 months ago, so it is refreshing to see one of my own kind again. They gave us tea, it being the C.C's custom to entertain all his subordinates when he is travelling. Tea over they departed to their own quarters, and later we joined up again for a good meal, interesting conversation, and an early bed. The following morning the two men spent most of the time together on local affairs, Colonial Office interest in Ashanti's well-being, and other West African news, while Mrs. Fuller and I wrote, read and talked; in fact it was a restful day for me as well as for her during their longish tour in the bush when away from the Fort. In the evening we all went to the Wesleyan school where the 70 odd children were ranged in rows, big ones at the back, and the little ones in front, the latter being very small and brown and fat with rolling eyes, and covered with bright cloths tied in a knot at the back. Six little girls had modelled cups and saucers from clay for our inspection. The Omanhin came in too, and leant nonchalantly against a post, some Mahommedan charms in a leather cord cocked at a rakish angle over his left eye with some linguists standing by. All this plus Moussa and Amadu Falani, our two policemen, in the company of a delightful and enormous untidy Amadu Grunshi, (the Fuller's orderly) an invaluable servant and a perfect dear. The children sang a hymn, and 'Rule Britannia', and Mr. Fuller wrote a little report in the school book. Rain came on violently, and we all fled to the rest-houses, Grunshi running beside me with an umbrella which he held over my head!

The Fullers next trek was one of some 23 miles, which meant an early start, dressing by candlelight, and having all the loads and beds, luggage, etc. ready by 7.0 a.m. David who had received a confession book by the last mail, was ready first, described himself in it as 'Melodramatic Martha' while Mr. Fuller, who was last, wrote of himself as 'a third rate Italian Tenor', very apt as he did sing in a good tenor voice. Mrs. Fuller and I got away first on foot at full steam along a splendid broad red highway through orchard country which rapidly became forestal. We passed one village where there were lots of donkeys from the North on their way to Sunyani for Kola nuts; the C.C. got into his hammock there, as did Mrs. Fuller a little later, but D. and I walked all the way as it was only 9 miles to the bank of the Tano which is the boundary of our District. We combined this conducting our Chief and his wife with the useful opportunity of planning a rest-house there, for quite often the river gets really wide, and makes the crossing almost impossible. The Tano is the most important Ashanti river, and also a sacred one; the village however is on the other side. There we parted from the Fullers who had another 14 miles before the next stop, and would be in thicker forest country most of the time.

We had a most unexpected treat in the village where, after crossing, we had to stay the night in order to give D. time for planning and arranging the position and size of the proposed rest-house. The linguist's house which had been cleaned out for us was not only a typical Ashanti house, but it had also an almost cobbled courtyard, made accidentally by generations of Kola nut epicures having thrown the shells out from the rooms around, and the nuts having sunk into the earth! A bright moon, very clear for a wonder after the heavy rains and mist of the last 3 or 4 days, lit up all the interiors while we sat there after dinner. Innumerable big bats flew squealing overhead and the low voices of the people mingled with the beating fu-fu—all of which acted as a soporific to us who were pretty tired, especially D. who had had to sit up late two nights running with the C.C. who is notorious as a late bedder, hardly ever before midnight! After the Fuller's departure, and our first crossing of the river, we had gone back to arrange for the marking out of the rest-house; while there we had admired the deep shady hollow in which the village stands, with tall palm trees, grass thatched houses, cocoa and banana trees, with people walking at that distance ($\frac{1}{2}$ mile) like little pigmies dwarfed by the great tall forest trees with their silver grey bark and greenery. It was higher too on that side, and the red rose up from the river which made it even more picturesque.

Today, December 8th, we fed the fish in their sacred river, and suceeded in getting one or two of them to show themselves by scattering some crumbs; Moussa had said they could be 'as large as men' in the Colony through which Tano finds its way to the sea, but here the ones we saw only seemed to be $\frac{1}{4}$-$\frac{1}{2}$ lb., a pale brown muddy colour with red tails, and fins like goldfish. The new rest-house programme having been dealt with, we walked back to the small village Kuntumso on the road to Tekiman again, spoke to the Chief for a few moments, and then saw Kofi Jesse, the old Tekiman linguist now terribly emaciated and thin—absolutely skeleton. David

greeted him warmly, and no wonder for he had been the sort
of Prime Minister at Tekiman for over 55 years, and was in
office during Sir Garnet Wolseley's 1874 campaign. He said
he had come for some medicine, and was wrapped in a red, white
and blue striped cloth. Kofi had a very fine and intelligent face,
and I wished we had been able to stay there a day or two, and
get him to pour out some of his reminiscences; as it was we
called for our chairs and sat down in the village street, while
Moussa stopped the carriers, and got hold of our medicine chest
out of which we produced some iron and arsenic tablets, one
being swallowed then with water out of a calabash, and another
given the old boy to be repeated tomorrow. This greatly
interested the villagers, but we had to get on, and were soon
passing donkeys and men with loads of Kola nuts in long wicker
baskets. These they supported in the fork of a tree when tired,
using the pole they walked with to prop up the other end. Added
to all this they generally have a straight sword slung over one
shoulder, and a dagger, and perhaps a couple of spears. We
had told the Omanhin beforehand not to receive us this time,
and the same to the Schoolmaster so we arrived at Tekiman
again quietly, and ready for luncheon.

The bright sunlight today gave the village quite a different
appearance than it had had when the C.C.'s party was here,
rows of red peppers spread on the ground to dry being particularly noticeable, and to me a brown small schoolchild giving
me a very smart salute from a doorway while clad simply in
nix! The terra cotta hue of the sandy earth helps as a background to the other sporadic colours and the greenery which
surrounds all the villages in this part of the District. After a
rest D. sought out the Omanhin, and while first administering
a stern reproof at finding the rest-house not cleaned up after
yesterday's departure (this the good sporting fellow took very
well) then showed him a very good photograph of himself taken
when we first entered the village on our way from Coomassie
to Wenchi, and which we had stuck in our photo album before
leaving Wenchi. The King was, when he realized that it was
himself, in peals of laughter and happiness—and wanted to
take it at once to his wife to see, but D. explained he would
have to get another print, and that it would be given him without fail to be kept by him in his family surroundings. Another

palaver of some kind took place, followed by the wild rush of our 'amacka boys' (as the hammock men are dubbed generally) to pull down the part of the old rest-house where we had slept, or tried to sleep, which was crumbling away and leaning over like the Tower of Pisa. After pulling and pushing the thatch off, and levering the walls with poles, the whole building collapsed one part after the other into tottering heaps of earth sending up red dust in clouds.

The following day, December 9th, I felt on awaking as if most of the starch had been taken out of me, aching limbs, head and eyeballs, on top of short broken slumber and slight fever seemed to predict malaria of some sort, but I wanted to accompany D. on a quick day trip to Tuobodom and back, so rather foolishly decided to go. When we were there some weeks previously, we had said that we would come back to inspect the new rest-house ordered on that occasion, so it being only a journey of 5 miles we started off with one hammock instead of our two, Osman on a bicycle, and Moussa with us walking. It was misty and damp, and at times a thick white blanket wrapped us round; the lean palm trees loomed like wraiths out of the whiteness! On the way at a small village, Osman enquired if there were any complaints on which a beefy looking fellow stood forward and said that he was a countryman of our Kakraba (a Krepi) who owed him £1 10s. upon which David said he could accompany us to Tekiman on our way back, where he could then settle the affair with Kakraba in court. To make up for their remissness last time, the Tuobodomites turned out in force and met us quite a long way from the town; the sword of State was borne in front of us, with calabashes covered with skins being used to create roaring noises, State umbrellas and all that, and we were rushed in great style to the new rest-house in its fine clearing, and jolly well built it was. Ashanti stools were produced for us, the seat part being leather, while the back and sides were covered with silver coins and nails. Having marked out places for windows to be made in the rooms, we held a friendly palaver, D. giving the people warm praise for their work, and answering various questions as to the C.C's visit and Ashanti news as a whole. We only spent about 25 minutes there, and returned to Tekiman as quickly as we could, my hammock boys' feet brushing through a carpet

of leaves as it is quite autumnal now and some trees almost bare.
Flowers however when seen are full of scent and bloom; they
are mostly white, one creeper especially sweet smelling—(a
cross between a syringa and a freesia?) though there are some
blue pea-like flowers as well. When we got back, we had hot
baths before lunch and then rested, but I seemed to feel more
and more feverish and ill, my teeth even rattling in the way
the Ashanti umbrellas rattle when carried alongside one's
hammock. Early bed, 5 grains of quinine, and a Wenchi cock-
tail ought to do the trick, and I hope to be a complete cure
tomorrow.

December 15th. Sadly unprophetic the last words I wrote!
Far from being well, I've been ill and have had six most unpleasant days. When I went to bed last Saturday night D.
had taken my temperature finding it romping gaily up, which
worsened during the next two days while I felt absolutely
rotten; meanwhile D. had sent a message 50 miles to Sunyani
telling Dr. Duff of my illness, and asking him to come to Wenchi
as soon as he could manage it, we ourselves to return there at
once so that I could at least be ill in more comfortable surroundings. The same evening we started after sunset, I tottering out
in pyjamas, and being wrapped up in a hammock carried most
carefully by our good permanent hammock boys. D. walked
beside me for the first 10 miles while I lay burning with fever
under the blankets, the night being fairly bright as the moon
rose soon after 7.30 behind the trees; the last few miles to
Nkwansia were agony, utter stillness in the bush except for the
pad-pad-pad of bare feet and the jog-jog of the hammock, a
kind of dream journey not quite as bad as a nightmare. A bed
had been sent on ahead to the rest-house which Mama who
had bicycled with one or two carriers had made ready for me—
it being the only thing on the earth floor of the one small room!
Once in it I had a cool drink, and David took my temperature
which no wonder had risen to 104.6. Luckily I went to sleep
for a bit which gave all the others time to push on to Wenchi,
while D. sent another note and some hammock boys to meet
Dr. Duff who had started from Sunyani within three hours of
receiving our message by Osman. The good clerk got back
dead tired having done 90 odd miles on a bicycle over grass-
grown bush paths, and damp patches; it is pretty difficult to

get help out here if ill when you are anything from 40-70 miles
from a doctor's H.Q., and even then perhaps find that he is
out in the other direction!

Once at Wenchi next morning I was quickly in my own bed,
and waited on; D. washing my face and hands, giving me soda
to drink and generally nursing me, Mama creeping about without a ghost of a smile on his usually merry little brown face.
When Dr. Duff first arrived he did not know whether I had
malaria or yellow fever, but by the next morning he pronounced
it malaria all right, and the temperature was dropping quite
rapidly; D. had made a cunning almost professional temperature chart which helped Duff. The yellow fever possibility is
always with us out here, but the attacks are rare though almost
always fatal to a man, but not in the case of a woman; in the
last epidemic 10 men and 1 woman got it, and *all* the men died.
For the first two days of Dr. Duff's arrival I had milk and soda
only—after that I began to want something better. Until today
bed was the order with an occasional period of sitting up, but
today I am up for the first real movement on my own after six
days of hardly enjoyable immobility. Duff's last order to me
was '15 grains of quinine daily for 3 more days, and then 5
grains daily till you go home'; I hate it, and it definitely makes
my ears feel deaf.

During my bout of malaria D. has been out one or two evenings with his gun, and yesterday for the first time this year saw
and bagged a greater bustard. They are very large birds, about
the size at least of a fine turkey, and awfully useful for the table.
This is the season for them, their lesser species, and many other
semi-migrant birds; it coincides with the strong and distasteful
'harmattan', a wind from the Sudan, hot and dry, and invoking
bad tempers much as the east wind does to us at home! I being
convalescent am rather over-teased by it, and have to watch
my reactions very carefully. Home news is not so bad, but one
wonders out here how a sort of coalition of Bonar Law and
Lloyd George will work, and one perhaps quite wrongly
deplores Asquith's resignation. The War and the constant news
as to casualties is worrying D. greatly. He has managed to write
in asking to be released to take up military service in Europe,
and had also consulted the C.C. when at Tekiman who
promised to back up his request, and at the same time will

inform the Colonial Office that he can administer Ashanti on a smaller cadre thus allowing younger men to serve in the forces if they wish to do so. As far as it concerns us, D. says he will resign if this permission is not granted by the end of January, but things may be different by then.

On December 18th I had a first walk in the town, where we had not been on inspection for at least three weeks. There apparently had been some cattle disease in the North, but the traffic had started again with two herds of the patient humped animals coming in while we were there. Back at our house D. became a doctor and administered several potions to Jakoba, one of our hammock boys who seemed to be quite sick and was looking very sorry for himself. Meanwhile one of the wives in the police barracks and the prison invited me to the name-day of a newly born babe, so attended by Moussa to interpret I went along. The child was a girl, the daughter of the warder. When I got there the mother of the week old babe was washing her outside the house, using one big calabash of water, one smaller one, and a piece of rough cloth; it was given a real good wash, and no noise about it either. I couldn't grasp how and when the name was given, and who named it, but seeing as I did a gash on its left cheeck I think that tribal mark was done privately, and the name produced at some moment of the marking; the child was called Halima. After inspection by me she was allowed to hold my finger which she promptly plunged into her mouth, at the same time lying rather like a pink rat squirming and naked. The police Sergeant (no relation) sat by in a Hausa robe, not uniformed, smiling beatifically at all of us; Moussa told me that he had fathered several children but they had all died young. Before leaving I got Moussa to interpret for me, and I blessed the child, and presented the mother with a string of beads for her, probably all the child's costume for some considerable time. In the afternoon one of the hammock boys working in the garden found and brought me a chameleon to see. We put it on the green felt tablecloth where it became a much brighter green, and then on a variegated bush green and yellow where it again immediately adapted its coat to its surroundings. They are ugly little animals with their large baggy mouths, spiny fronts, and rolling beady eyes.

On December 21st, Mr. Pott, the Provincial Commissioner

of this part of Ashanti turned up, on a visit to see how the town has grown, and also to give David a law exam; these extra necessities of knowledge, of which languages are the most important, have to be passed at certain periods by all the Civil Servants while out here, as transfers and promotions are affected by the results, and also the suitable district or office where a Commissioner is needed. D. was quite capable of passing the verbal part, and scored 90%, but in the written he could do very little—and no wonder, one of the questions being 'If a man proposed to the wrong girl in the dark, could she sue for breach of promise!' One could hardly imagine a more stupid question in an examination out here—so much for red tape!

Mr. Pott left for Sunyani on the 23rd and it is now Christmas Eve, but I feel more like Good Friday, being at the moment plagued with a sore throat, aches and pains, and a bad cold (probably the best African type of influenza!) but it will pass— the beastly Harmattan wind is responsible. On last Friday one Moshi stabbed another in the neck, and yesterday a man hung himself, probably out of spite; that seems to be all that has happened recently. This morning soon after I got up, Mama presented me with a large sheet of foolscap, on which was printed in red and blue letters of immense size the following letter:—

Miss Boyle                                    Prison Office, Wenchi.
Herewith sending you 2 fowl, 11 eggs for Christmas present. I wish you Merry Christmas and Happy New Year.
                                             W. G. Akaton,
Wenchi.                          K.O.P. (Keeper of Prison)

It was rather nice of the gaoler, poor man; I feel quite sorry for him as he is a Coast man and hates being up here, also he is alone for his equally coastified wife won't come to the Wilds with him! I sent him a note of thanks, and a little 1917 Calendar I happened to have.

Most of the afternoon was spent in tying up presents for the faithful Staff, an operation made easier and more exciting as Mother had sent me a whole roll of bright blue ribbon to work with. Shirts, ties, collars, pocket knives, head scarves, beads, a toy field gun, torches, a sheep (*not* tied with blue ribbon!) for the Police Sergeant, cummerbands for the 12 hammock boys, puttees for the two postmen, and many feminine things for the wives and girl children; it was a pretty strenuous three or four hours, and we managed it unseen as between meal times we also put up a large sized model of Santa Claus. This was followed by a brief walk round the nearest farms to try for a bird or two, but no luck. Home before our dinner and a short service it being both Sunday and Christmas Eve; we then each hung a stocking for the other, in order that we could perform the traditional Santa Claus visit—D. had told Mama that S.C. would come in the night, and fill the stockings which of course happened! and when we were called on Christmas morning, it was by Mama's peals of laughter when he found the stockings full of oranges and little packages for each other, as for example an ivory hand mirror in my stocking, and a silver shoehorn in D.'s. Mama's interest and excitement lasted so long that he was hardly able to pull up the mosquito nets which is his first morning job. Outside it was cool and fresh with the red light of the rising sun shining into the rooms, and a thick dew on the grass. Before and during breakfast we produced and played with automatic toys like the moving of a plate by pressing a rubber bulb, firing little squibs from toy pistols—a game that made the hammock boys outside yell with laughter. We told the Staff to clear breakfast, and leave us alone for a short time, so that while they were busy in the background we could cover the tables with the presents and dispose of the cardboard Santa Claus we had made and displayed yesterday. Then the whole Staff, Police, hammock boys, Osman and all wives were summoned, and got their presents with smiles, and constant 'Alberka's'—real thanks and happiness.

We had had all the flags put up on the flagpole and some smaller posts, arranged for games, football and running to be got up by the police and the other employees, and gave a free pass to the village and Zongos to drum and generally amuse themselves until 9.0 p.m.—At midday we tackled an enormous turkey we had bred from one a previous Provincial Commissioner had given us from his little fowl run at Sunyani. A rest in the afternoon gave us time to have a nice personal Christmas Service with 'Hark the Heralds' and other familiar hymns followed by tea with mince pies, ginger and preserved fruits out of the Fortnum store cupboard. It was my first Christmas away from home, but I enjoyed it enormously, and I feel sure this was the case with all the boys, police and others, and will be a day to be remembered by them, especially by Ali, Mama and Tani who loudly lamented the departure of the old man 'Tsofo daria—who laughed' as we at home lament the passing of St. Nicholas.

Boxing Day found us all rather worn out after the unusual dissipation of Christmas Day, which is just as well for the harmattan wind blows hotter and hotter, and the cool inside rooms of the house more and more tempting. D. went down to the Court as usual, and I was 'bunched' by the police Sergeant who sent me an enormous bunch of bananas quite green which one can hang up to ripen. There is a rumour of some elephants in the neighbourhood, so Moussa was sent off to try and get definite news about this, while after acknowledging the home mail letters and presents we took a tour round some of the farms looking for 'fakara'. Believe it or not, the very first farm produced a brace not far from me and I dropped one stone dead with my left barrel! There were shouts of joy and of 'ja faddi'—he is fallen, on the strength of which I was asked by the policeman with us to get a pass given for the village in honour of my 'bindiga' (gun) to have bands and dancing until 9.0 p.m. which I succeeded in doing for him.

The last five days of 1916 have been comparatively uneventful, but we were able to do one or two things useful and rather interesting. On December 28th we spent one day at Nkwansia taking the midday meal with us to the rest-house there, while D. with Osman, some police and all the hammock boys laid out and helped to install the fencing in of a cattle kraal with old telegraph wire; this has been sent us from Sunyani to use in that way. Being only 5 miles from Wenchi on the main road via Coomassie, it is good policy to maintain a cattle kraal there and reduce the sometimes excessive number of animals waiting in the Wenchi Zongos. I took (borrowed) a large black umbrella, a 'Blackwood's' and a 'Saturday Review' to browse over in the rest-house, while the Commissioner and his Staff got down to the work in the early part of the day; having started soon after 7.0, they managed to carry on from 9.0–12.0, and after a rest had the marking out completed, and the wiring started by 4.30, so we got back to Wenchi soon after 6.0, having done a good

day's work. It was a hazy still evening with the setting sun like
a round red sovereign, and no blaze or coloured clouds as in
the wet or more ordinary weather; the harmattan affects
conditions here much as a similar wind does in the Red Sea or
Persian Gulf—or perhaps more particularly in Egypt or the
Sudan. Next day D. had a great deal of end of the year work
and reports to do in the Courthouse, so I spent it on very
domestic chores in doing which I noticed not for the first time
how this climate destroys crepe-de-chine or satin—all tear
quickly, while the books in the bookcases tend to dry up and
bend over. This is really worse than the usual green mould in
the rains, for that can be wiped off continually. We spent the
30th at another village on the Northern Territories road, and
tried for and saw some bustards, but couldn't get near them.
Moussa came back reporting the elephant rumour was correct,
as he actually saw the footprints, but although he also unexpectedly saw three bongos in the flesh it was not possible for
us to get that far without making a camp there. This we must
try to do early in 1917.

Meanwhile I write this in the evening of December 31st
1916, and our first five months in West Africa end accordingly.

# CHAPTER VII

# Transfer to Ejura

In the bound copy of my original Diary there is a little coloured drawing of myself being carried 'in' and almost tumbling 'out' of my hammock; it may be that I meant it to signify tumbling into the New Year! Actually it was a pleasant morning which I spent on domestic affairs in the house and the garden, while D. with Osman was counting £150 in shillings at the Courthouse. Tani who was helping me with the laundry informed me that she and Mama are going to be married during the next two days, and I was delighted to hear the news. They are such nice children 16 perhaps and 13 respectively but they are making a real love match which is a very rare thing out here; they both have worked for D. since early in 1915, so they make a perfect team, and enjoy every moment of their housework and of the travelling. Apparently the ceremony and all the excitements last two days during which they personally have got very little to do with it, and the cost is about £3 10s., largely presents for (*not* from) the mallams and friends, kola nuts, scent and little things, all of which Ali (the cook) and Moussa (the orderly) were to see about in the town this morning. David has given the whole village and Zongos a pass for noise i.e. bands, singing, dancing and gun firing until 10.0 p.m. both days. This is an important decision from the young married's point of view as they would 'get shame' if things were not done in a big way, and the music and dancing ranks highest on these occasions.

It was a dull grey afternoon, the Omanhin sending us a New Year's present of a large fat sheep, yams and other edibles in the hands (or mostly on the heads) of his own people. This was

85

announced by Moussa who also came to inform us of the details and ceremonial of the wedding; meanwhile both the affianced go on with their normal tasks as if nothing new was happening. After dark there was a watery moon gleaming aloft which encouraged us to sit on the verandah steps and listen to the terrific volume of noise from the town below. The rhythmical drumming and tinkling of the Jimini band including the calabash shaken full of beans roared up to us in some of the gusts of wind, as also did the choruses of the men and the shrill voices of the younger girls but it was perfectly continuous and steady; at times it was as if an enormous organ had all its stops full out, and then suddenly dying away with a faint tap of drums and a murmuration of voices. It made us realize that all our servants and people were happy and that we love and care for them, they loving us in return. The police sergeant is quite adorable, and actually begged me to accept the only photograph he had of himself taken at Coomassie with the police there. I said he must keep it for his house, but was very flattered at his offer.

Tani, the bride, was taken next afternoon to the Mallam's house, with Ali's wife Asetu, and Moussa acting for the non-existent father and mother as appears to be the custom. We decided that we would go and make an extended tour of the town, including inspection of the cattle kralls, market, and Zongos. This would also give us some sort of guidance of the wedding procedure, so we summoned the sergeant to attend us, Moussa being wedding-employed; this pleased him and he wasted no time (except that his own clock was 20 minutes slow!), and we started off by picking off a few green pigeons near the Courthouse—and then came across a really large drove of cattle, some 200, just in from the North. Bodammassie, for that is the sergeant's name, is not only amusing but also a very intelligent man; D. described his quarters in the police lines to me for he saw them in inspection. There was a table in the middle of the room with a china soup tureen and a covered china vegetable dish on it, and on a shelf a Nuttall's English Dictionary and two signalling manuals—it seemed to me to pair very well with what I saw in some of the houses in the town, a dusky figure wrapped in a robe pedalling away at a Singer sewing machine, of which several are sold at the village store! After a brief look round the town for it was getting late, we passed by Mallam Nadaka's house where our little bride was temporarily immured. Outside all the young girls were dancing their peculiar dance singing and clapping their hands, and jumping one another in the air while two or three men drummed. Further on some small boys were giving a display of step-dancing accompanied by a drum and an old kerosene tin beaten with a piece of metal. We paused there for a short time, and then made our way home via a compound in which were the most attractive donkeys of dusky grey, brown and very dark brown almost black in fact.

While we were sitting at dinner and Mama was away to the kitchen for another course, we heard the beating of a quaint little hand drum or two coming nearer, mingled with the shouts and laughter of girls and women. This was the return of the bride. We ran to our bedroom in order to look out and could just see a long line of figures passing across the grass to the boys' houses. Once there, they assembled and the play went on, singing, clapping of hands, plenty of talk, noise and clatter. Meanwhile the bridegroom pursued his vocation as butler with the greatest unconcern except for an occasional giggle. The man has no part nor lot in these proceedings. David suggested that I should go and see Tani upon which Mama was sent to call Asetu, one of Ali's wives—and I was escorted by her to the house where the girls were sitting in a circle outside. Stooping under the low thatched roof I went in with Asetu to the room which was crowded as much as the space admitted with girls of Tani's age or thereabouts. Fatima, another older wife, was sitting at a little table on which there was one lighted candle, and I looked round for Tani, finally spotting a funny little figure among the group, sitting on the floor, and hidden under a white muslin veil. Asetu raised the veil, and displayed a very shy and rather nervous looking Tani, her black wool all frizzed out, and her nice little brown body naked. She looked such a very small child. I kissed her on the forehead and said 'Yanzu ak yi amre, ka samu miji mi kyean'—'Now that you are married, you have found a good husband'; great applause. The veil was then thrown over Tani's face again, and I returned to the pudding course! In about half an hour with the tip-tap-tap-tap of the drum and the shrill tremolo voices of the youthful

female friends cutting the still evening air, the bridal party
wended its way back to the town leaving Tani in what has
been her home for a good long time, and the marriage is a
natural result. It is very interesting to have seen something of
a real proper official wedding out here as it doesn't often fall
to one's lot to be actually in it so to speak.

All this was just in time, for the very next day January 3rd
the overdue mail arrived with a despatch transferring us to
Ejura and stating that our relief would arrive almost at once.
It will be an awful wrench leaving Wenchi, and I was quite
upset by the sight of the sergeant's horror-struck face when he
heard the news; and his pathetic 'Who is coming here?' The
servants are dreadfully sorry too as Wenchi is a very popular
spot, and it has become almost a Euro-African affair for David
has really made it what it is, and all the inhabitants seem to
regard him as a permanent godfather and court of appeal.
Anywhere it is sad uprooting oneself, but this is a wandering
life and we must take it cheerfully. Ejura is a more important
post both physically and politically, and was a key position
in the Ashanti world two hundred years ago; now for our value
it has one great change, a motor road from Coomassie 70 miles
away which means one step nearer home! For the next six
days we were up to our eyes in directing the packing, dismantling our rooms, collecting carriers, and deciding how to dispose
of gear which would no longer be useful, including provisions
from our store cupboard. Our successor Mr. Cutfield was
supposed to be somewhere on the way, and his first batch of
carriers arrived almost at once. This made it easier to arrange
transport for our possessions, and we in fact sent off the first
batch on January 7th in charge of one of the policemen, Amedu
Fulani, some 13 or 14 cases packed with glass, china, stores,
books and three tin uniform cases as well. The chop boxes being
all the same size vary of course according to what is in them,
and it amused me to watch the line of carriers on tip-toe, until
the order 'forward to your load' was given, trying to figure out
which looked heavy, and which light! Books and bedding were
obviously not to be carried at all costs.

D. has been busy most days with criminal returns and official
papers, for it is the week for sending in the annual report, and
now in addition there is preparation for handing over. Still he

found time to arrange one or two gifts to Osman (the clerk), for example a box holding syphons and fitted up for that, and a few surplus tins of food here and there. Besides that we are making up some of our Fortnum stores for sale to Doctor Duff at Sunyani who is running very short there, while we can always replenish our store cupboard at Ejuna by car in a few hours. As recreation was needed we organized one evening a free-for-all football match in the compound, my side against D.'s in which the staff, the police, the hammock boys, Osman and other odd chaps, rushed about, pirouetting on one leg, shouting in Hausa, Moshi and English with the greatest joy and the most sportsmanlike manner—even in one occasion after a goal was disallowed shouting 'Allah ya ba mun woni'— 'God will give us another'. Rather unlike Rangers and Celtic at Hampden! The same evening just before sunset I saw something moving in the cut grass over the garden fence, and drew D's attention to it; he leapt up from his writing, ran to his dressing room and came back with his gun, while Mama and I restrained Hankuri (who followed a gun automatically). David then stepped round the house—stalked behind some barbadoes pride bushes—and suddenly rising up managed to down the bird first shot; it was a greater bustard, generally regarded as the biggest game bird there is. It was a magnificent specimen measuring 6 ft. 9 ins. from tip to tip of the wings and when stretched out stood four feet from beak to feet; the wings were enormous, brown and white, and it seemed a shame to kill it, but the bird is most excellent eating and would give us a welcome change from the usual rather tough meat obtainable in the market. We had been expecting the annual bustard (greater and lesser) migrants for some time, and they obviously had now arrived in our part in strength, we having seen two of the smaller ones already in the farms beyond the village.

On January 8th Cutfield arrived, and for the next four days D. and he were working together, inspecting the town, going through correspondence, official reports, cash and furniture lists with Osman at the Court, meeting the various chiefs and local personages; in fact, handing over. I spent most of that time making my own personal preparations for departure and superintending the final packing with the boys, when I suddenly realized while we were dining with Cutfield on January 12th that we were indeed saying goodbye to our first own home, and I heard for the last time the Jimini band playing in the village below as they had done so often every week.

It is now late afternoon at Nkwansia where I am recording the last moments of our five months at Wenchi, having arrived there on August 16th and left it rather sadly this morning January 13th. The day was damp, and misty so we weren't tempted to look at views or see whether the garden still flourished; we had to say goodbye to all that, and after an early breakfast, a final collection of remnants, and the despatch in front of us of the carriers partly transport ones (Mendis who had come with Cutfield—the rest being our own Moshis) we left the bungalow soon after 9 o'clock escorted by all the police to the end of the town.

The Omanhin, the Jimini, Wangara, Moshi and Hausa chiefs were all waiting to say goodbye to us at the far end of the market, where we stopped to say our farewells to them, while David made a short address of friendship and thanks with a hope that they would all progress and succeed as before. Meanwhile the police were all shaking hands with Moussa; Osman who in a letter to D. signs himself as 'Your dear boy' is coming with us to Tekiman so as to serve us till the last moment. Once started, we in spite of a slight choky feeling of sadness walked the well known five miles to this rest-house at a pretty good pace, being ensconced here in chairs and reading the last mail's home papers by 11 o'clock.

In the afternoon we took a stroll along a patch we'd not seen before which led us to the hill from which the Wenchi tribe believe they came into the world, as after a large cavity had opened out of which came a man and nine children the ninth one called 'No more', and the cavity closed. This belief was perpetuated in the custom of sacrificing the ninth child to the Tribal fetish as being the cause of the tribe not being greater in numbers, and it has existed ever since, with occasional instances of the demanded sacrifice as for example in 1915 when one occurred about 11 miles away from Wenchi. Osman and some police were sent off at once followed by D. who held an enquiry there and then, as soon as the facts and the circumstancial details had been investigated by Osman and the police sergeant, the fetish priest and his wife were arrested and

immediately sent for trial to Coomassie on the charge of murder.
The verdicts there being 'guilty', they were sentenced to death
but Sir Hugh Clifford the Governor wisely (he had great
knowledge of both Oriental and African tribal histories and
native religions) commuted the sentence to 20 years imprisonment for the man, and exile to the Coast for his wife. At the
same time H.E. ordered all Officers in the government to
explain the case in detail to the people in every District and
forbid it once and for all under certain death penalty.

January 14th our last Sunday in the District, and swallowing
an early breakfast we were well on the way by 6.45 in a thick
mist. Before long we met Amedu Fulani returning from Ejura
where he had safely delivered the first company of carriers, and
was now instructed to accompany us as it was advisable to have
another policeman to help Moussa who was the only one with
us, and the carriers often have to be sent on ahead for their
journey is subject to periods of rest. Our arrival at Tekiman
took us through the Zongo and the main village the Omanhin
tearing up in his usual business-like fashion to receive us at the
rest-house, and then go on with his stool bearers and elders to
the Court for a short palaver. He is the funniest fellow I've
struck this side of the Equator and bursting with personality,
and is much upset by our departure as he feels that D. has
always kept him strong in his position, and upheld his own
judgements in front of his people. We too feel that he has done
a lot in reverse and has made his people in the outlying villages
recognize in D. a Commissioner who looks after them all.

Rather tired after the very busy days of clearing up at
Wenchi, we spent the remainder of the day in having one usual
little service together, then strolling in the market and the
Zongo where we found a great number of the handsome and
happy donkeys, some rolling in the dust and other hobbling
along in the grass; they liked being petted and having their
ears pulled, and they behaved like creatures accustomed to
strangers and obviously well cared for. An early bed as tomorrow's journey might well be a long and tiring one found us fast
asleep when somewhere round midnight the noisiest and quite
most terrifying thunderstorm broke with an hour or two of
lightning in every direction, and ending finally with rain and
wind that swamped everything before stopping as suddenly as

it had begun. The faithful Mama appeared with a lantern at the commencement of this tornado, and crept around seeing all was safe right to the end. On awaking properly about 6 a.m. D. decided that the road and the bush paths would be impossible for the carriers, who would only stumble along and fall perhaps in thick slippery mud breaking cases with crockery or other contents; so it was agreed not to leave Tekiman today at all. We and the servants gratefully applauded this and turned over to sleep again until rising for breakfast at almost 9 a.m. and then spending the morning on letters and books plus another talk with our friend the chief. This was followed in the brighter and clean smelling afternoon by a walk round farms and patches of forest, getting a good idea of the surroundings as a whole which when travelling on duty one did not always take in. The prospects looked good, and we retired after dinner hoping for a fine day tomorrow.

And it was one; January 16th Tuesday opened with a clear rising sun and an early start, literally fleeing from the ubiquitous escort of schoolchildren who chose on this occasion to speed us with a raucous rendering of 'shall we meet beyond the river?' sung over and over again! After about ten minutes of this David felt we could really stand it no longer, as the faster our hammock men went so the faster did the schoolchildren run; at a suitable moment he stopped his men and getting out of the hammock walked back to the teacher who was with the children, thanked him profusely for the farewells they were giving, and suggested that this was far enough. So everyone was pleased and after a further half mile or so in hammocks we got out and walked, as was our normal custom for the first seven to eight miles if the weather was good. It was rather a typical country of the more really tropical kind. Before we got to Forekum, still a Tekiman village, there was a curious outcrop of great grey rocks and boulders which gave the scrubbily wooded country quite a different complexion; after that the path is more enclosed, and the day hotter so I delayed no longer but got back into my hammock which today had the Mendi crew, all experts from the Coast who carry their passengers not only swiftly but in complete comfort. I had just noticed some pineapples growing in a small clearing beside the path when we emerged into a large bush village of rather sprawling red-walled and thatched houses, quite unsophisticated as the inhabitants not being in a main road were interested at once. Up came the chief, whom I directed behind me to D. who was still walking—and when he arrived we both sat under the central big tree and had some drinks from our Thermos flasks; I showed the chief the hot-cork which astonished him no end! Just at the same moment a policeman from Ejura appeared with a note from Alec Norris, the outgoing Commissioner—this, as we had been travelling along and under the telegraph wire ever since Tekiman, made me feel back in the world somehow. Another hour and we were once more in Nkoranza and its modern rest-house, a 3-roomed corrugated-iron monstrosity!

We had spent a night here five months previously on our way to Wenchi from Coomassie, and then had met the young king who came to greet us again soon after we arrived this time. His mother the old Queen Mother (a recognized rank among the Ashanti tribes) had been particularly loyal to us in 1900 although in great difficulties as regards some of her people; but she had managed to keep them quiet and thus had contributed valuable influence throughout the country at the critical moment. Still alive, she rules behind the scenes as is the Ashanti custom, in case as often happens the chosen and titular king is weak or unpopular. During the 1900 crisis her loyalty probably saved the lives of Captain Parmeter, Major Morris, and other officers at Kintampo where there was a large quantity of valuable stores on which several of the smaller tribal chiefs had kept a covetous eye.

After tea we wended our way to the telegraph office entering it for the first time since we had seen one at Coomassie in early August! The line goes from here to Kintampo, but has not yet reached Wenchi where it must soon penetrate as the cattle market there badly needs more rapid communication with the coast markets. Here it is a small thatched shanty with printed notices on the door, and inside telegraph forms, calendars and a very nice fat native clerk—all rather like a small office at the end of an Highland pier except for the tiny bush cat 'Abrebeia' that the clerk was holding in his arms! It was the sweetest thing like a small kitten with a long thick ring-streaked tail, a pointed head, a long snout, and keen little grey-green eyes. I soon had it in my arms while a small group of Ashantis looked on very interested, and I was able to ask the Omanhin's linguist questions as to its mode of life. It apparently feeds on bananas, and had just eaten a bit of one. They grow as large as our big wild cats, and when older can bite and scratch very badly. The postmaster wished to present it to me, but although I really did want to accept, the difficulty was that one was travelling; but it was very nice of the owner to offer it spontaneously.

There were three Reuters banging up above the telegraph desk, one with the news of the battleship 'Cornwallis' being torpedoed in the Mediterranean with fortunately only 13 of her personnel lost. Back in the rest-house a sick carrier with a strained leg was brought in order to show us it was a genuine case, a Nkoranza man with a swollen leg came up with a complaint (vocal *not* medical) which D. settled satisfactorily, and the Omanhin's linguist came to see the hornets nest in one of the rest-house rooms so that he could remove it after our departure! Then bed, as we have to do a 25-26 mile march tomorrow through a certain amount of rather trackless country. Long and partly trackless it was, looking back on it from Secheredumase where we arrived at about 3.15 p.m. on Wednesday January 17th having left Nkoranza at 6.30 a.m. with but one stop of an hour on the way. It was quite pretty country, open forest for the most part but little life and only one village, though one knows that somewhere (even quite close at times) there are small farms and habitations, if only bush headquarters for the local hunters whose Dane guns ensure meals of meat on occasions. Tomorrow it will be some 17 miles to Ejura through a part of the country as yet quite unknown to either of us.

Thursday January 18th. The cross country journey is complete, for we are now in our new home, the D.C's house at Ejura, after an interesting but rather swampy and forest ridden march, which suddenly ended by the sight of a hill in front of us with a bungalow on the top of it! We realized then that we were looking at the Ejura scarp, the termination of the Coomassie road which had only been finished some two years ago; it was splendidly made by the Sappers whose work is always first class. Alec Norris met us when we crossed the road (the house is 1½ miles short of Ejura itself) and soon hammocks, carriers, ourselves and all the staff were in the large compound which here accommodates the District Commissioner. It is magnificently sited on the spur of the hill with views for miles over the forest country to the west, and a sort of private view of the road some 60 feet below where anything or anybody arriving or leaving is well within sight. The house is a big barn-like building with a shingle roof, shuttered windows, an excellent pillared verandah on the side above the road, and a big almost uncared for garden and extensive compound with odd huts and sheds, which rather naturally have had little attention from our bachelor predecessor. Not even the pantry had shelves, and I soon realized I'd have plenty to do!

After lunch which Alec had ready for us, we unpacked a bit and tried to get things shipshape, one particular problem being the moving of a large bed out of the main bedroom so as to make use of our two camp beds that accompany us everywhere. To do this we not only had to remove a door but even one of the shutters on the verandah; re-arrangement seemed to have been unusual in this old fashioned house. At tea time Norris, who had moved himself to a small round house in the compound, came along to take us round the garden and surrounding land which boasted a chicken kraal, a vegetable garden (in which he had grown some jolly good cucumbers), and a splendid spring of clear water gushing out of the rock on which all this is situated. Later on the Omanhin and representatives of the other Ashanti Chiefs in the District with the Zongo leaders accompanied by three horsemen, and the usual coloured umbrellas and smart clothes, came to welcome the incoming Commissioner, so by dinner time we were at any rate accepted and housed. An early bed was the motto; surrounded by unpacked loads we soon fell into a dreamless sleep.

Next day Alec went off with D. to the village for the whole morning in order to start handing over, inspect the village lay-out and generally pass on information and experience of the place to his successor. There is a good deal to get to know at the beginning of taking over a new District, and Ejura with its important Headquarters on the road to the Northern Territories has several problems which a place like Wenchi would not have to deal with. Before going Alec rushed into

me saying I was an angel, and 'could I look at *these*, and do
the best I could for them?' *These* were a bundle of the worst
holes-in-heel and torn socks that I've ever seen or imagined;
to begin with they took a good quarter of an hour to 'pair' them,
then that or more to come to a verdict on them, and finally I
managed to make three pairs just but only just wearable, the
rest having to be got rid of at once! This is rather typical of the
isolated single officers, much as the housekeeping side of their
lives must be. The tablecloth is left on all day; in the middle
of it there is a bottle of Worcester sauce, a glass jar of brilliant
yellow butter, various receptacles with pepper, salt and
mustard together with at least two whisky advertisements
inscribed ash trays. The very chairs are cobwebby, the stores
are kept in old boxes in a big room with no table or shelves to
put them on, and in fact none of the modest refined comforts
of life are available or apparently even required. This under-
lines the view of the majority of men out here which is that
they don't believe in women coming out to the Coast and they
don't want them; they'd only get ill, and be a nuisance. Even
if they do come out as I now have, and Mrs. Fuller for example,
they are politely received but always with the sort of suppressed
view 'Poor beggar, it's a pity she is here but, come on, let's be
kind to her!' In the Coast towns Accra, Cape Coast, etc. it is
rather different for they can be packed off home easily—but
even then they are not so far really wanted. Even allowing for
the difficulties of the war, and the comparatively short time
since 1900 and the taking over of Ashanti, it seems to me obvious
that the usual cry at home of 'NO, don't go near the West
Coast, you'll die either of fever or drink' has up to now affected
the recruiting; that means there are not enough of the voca-
tional type of officers, who like the I.C.S. would bring not only
brains and leadership but also by their wives comfort, culture,
and the feminine example which Africans are ready to learn
about and appreciate. Alec, who is very frank and straight
spoken is completely anti-women out here, Philbrick at Coomassie with more experience thought them perhaps a burden,
Captain Armitage only if they were 'Sporting' and had no
fears of illness or native life—Ross however approved of them
if carefully selected, etc. But there it is; David thinks that one
of these days the right medium and satisfactory balance will be

found, but it may be too slow in coming while the African's present adolescence may by then have merged into leadership for themselves and no longer satisfaction with European rule in the outposts.

After yesterday's conversational evening, for that is what this question of white women out here turned into, we were by no means both to have a quiet home Saturday. Part of the morning was spent in arranging our own possessions and supervising the unpacking and checking of the stores, china, glass, books and clothes we had brought with us; after a late luncheon and a little rest hour it was the careful inspection and planning of the garden that needed our decisions. We accompanied by Moussa and the hammock boys arranged for immediate cutting back of the grass, digging of more vegetable beds, tidying the excellent pineapple section and then sitting down to a comfortable tea in the loggia which is formed by the stone parapet on the edge of the cliff, the white pillars of the verandah on that side of the bungalow, and the shade of one or two tall trees that grow on the cliff shading the southern rays of the sun.

This quiet Saturday afternoon enjoyment was furthered by the arrival with Alec, who had been completing his office files, of Mr. Migeod the Transport Officer, who comes up here in his car from Coomassie for weekends and an odd day or two in order to keep his eye on the carriers, troops, officers, and other persons proceeding to or returning from the Northern Territories. That part of the Gold Coast Governor's administration is an area bigger than Ashanti with very open plains, and a large river (the Volta) and several ranges of hills, and is rather sparsely populated. It has always acted as a buffer between the Coast ruled by us and the French territories to the West and North, the purely Mahommedan tribes to the North and North-East, and down to the Coast again the Germans in their single Togoland Colony.

Migeod is not only extremely able in his transport administration but is a good linguist, full of knowledge as to the African life, the tribal differences, and what not-to-do; full of humour he is always ready to help and advise anyone who comes along and requires it. Before he had been with us half an hour, we had somehow become a small party of white people full of life, fun, and interesting topics; no wonder we insisted on both of them remaining to dine with us, although they had both to leave early.

The next day Sunday 21st the Zongo people arrived to build a small house in the compound, and as at Wenchi the ones here believed in 'Music while you work' and had an amusing mixture of a wooden horn with a note like that of a cow, another one which had a monotonous plaintive sound, a few small hand drums and the leader playing a little motif over and over again on about six notes in a minor key. Meanwhile the workers carried up large bundles of grass for the roof, brought sticks and 'ti-ti' for the framework and, while some put up the walls weaving smaller sticks and pliant branches in and out, the rest made the conical shaped roof to be thatched with grass. From 11 o'clock onwards there was much writing of letters, a little service of our own followed by the African Sunday luncheon of ground nut to which Alec came, and then a bit of shut-eye. Migeod and Alec left next day, and I was left alone in the morning with gardening jobs, house and all that; Moussa stays with me here, for it is unlike Wenchi, the village or town being over 1½ miles away and the Court, Clerk, prison, police barracks, and rest-house all being together near the village on the main road. Also the method of running things here is traditional, and our way of village inspection, even court work, at Wenchi was adopted to meet conditions there; here it would be odd and rather embarrassing if accompanied by Moussa I did an inspection of village markets, Zongos, etc., by myself.

But I am already finding out that one will not be long alone, for about 4 o'clock Moussa suddenly appeared and said 'White man come', and sure enough a good Scot from Aberdeen, one of the Doctors, appeared and made himself known to me. He was on his way to Gambaga in the N.T. which is a 22 day's marching from here, and delighted to meet another Scot on the way. Dr. Goodbrand, for that was his name, was only just out from home and made the most of our meeting by not only enjoying scones for tea (which luckily I had ordered anyhow) but was able to get a good talk with D. about conditions out here. He went back to the rest-house about half past six, having bicycled up from there, and will be leaving as early as possible tomorrow morning, for with the Harmatan rather strong just now any forced march after midday is very hot work. I heard hyenas howling mournfully through the night, one quite near, and indeed Moussa saw tracks in the pineapple grove next morning. It suddenly struck me that I'd now been here five days and had never seen Ejura itself, so this evening January 24th after tea in the cool D. walked down with me along the flat red road first to the official houses and compounds where I met Mensah, the nice Fanti clerk, and the police sergeant, warden and others—and then after another ¼ mile the Ashanti village with the Zongos at the North end, at least two miles from our house.

We were hardly back at our own bungalow when another case of 'White man come' required our attention and it turned out to be Alec back again bringing with him a Mr. Rosenthal who has come out from home to cinematograph Ashanti! They had come up from Coomassie to Mampong 26 miles South of us to arrange details with the Chief there who is the most important in the country and of the real Royal blood, and Alec thought it would be a good thing to come on and discuss it here first, David now being the D.C. in whose District Mampong is. Mr. Rosenthal is a most extraordinary man. He was a chemist and had been for some years at St. George's Hospital, and with another man had invented some sort of cinematography some time ago. Apart from that he had been in Peking in the 1900 Boxer rising and in the Philippines, Port Arthur, Egypt, India, Burma, North and South America, but never before this in Africa, West or South.

In appearance he was of the heavy Jewish build with iron grey hair and a dark moustache, age nearing 50, and tho' he was a rough diamond of the cockney type (dropped his h's inevitable) and stammered, he seemed a straight nice-thinking person. He told me that as soon as he landed on the Coast he could see what was wrong with West Africa, 'drink' and the lack of women to help things along. This naturally pleased me, but it is interesting that two persons (he and I) should form the same opinion on their first visit; new comers often see or feel most of the game. He told us the latest news i.e. that there has been quite serious trouble in Northern Nigeria where the Senussi have come right across Africa and wiped out two French posts and one English one; he also told us that the Marine Bandmaster of the W.A.F.F. at Coomassie died the other day.

Alec has applied for a Commission there, and he hopes he'll succeed as the C.O. at H.Q. has backed it up strongly. It was arranged before they left us that we should go down to Mampong on Friday and meet them there so as to see the war dance and the photographing. D. of course approves of this plan, especially as it enables him to meet the Omanhin which he should do at once on taking over the District; to me the plan was as exciting as having an afternoon off at school, and going out to tea with a relative or friends! So next day (Thursday January 25th) we would be on the road South, and by motor car not hammocking for the first time in this District.

Easier written than done! It is now well on in the day (in fact, after a late breakfast) on which we were supposed to start, as during the final hours of the night an absolutely incredible storm blew up which for over three hours kept everyone awake and frightened to death by lightning flashing through the bungalow under our beds with roars of thunder non-stop. Simultaneously plus rain coming down in perpetual force like a solid sheet of liquid. Somehow we all, and the building, survived and D. and I are now drying ourselves and looking out things to pack quickly so as to get away in Migeod's car which he has lent us for our little trip; it means only two servants and a sort of 24 hours picnic, but it isn't easy quite to pick out the right necessaries. Apart from that, most of our clothes and anything in the rooms were and are soaked with the rain with a mist which lasted until nearly midday. But having despatched a lorry with kit and servants, we managed to push off, and saw for the first time the country and the new road as well as the Afram river in flood at one point. The sappers had done their job so well that they even provided manholes for the daily groups of carriers to rest in with shaped wooden rests for the loads, and a cleared space for donkeys or other animals; but some of the Northern tribesmen still prefer the old road (or track!) which crosses from one side of the new one to another at intervals.

It was approximately 4 o'clock when we arrived at Mampong which to me with its European stores, a Basel Mission and school, a church with a spire, appeared to be a real town as if we were no longer in the 'bush'; this feeling was intensified by the fact that the rest-house is in the middle of the town, and has no privacy or quiet seclusion of its own. We slept in a mosquito-proof room (a kind of cage within a room), but it was all rather dirty and unkempt; there was one blessed thing about it, and that was we did not hear a cheep from the town after 9.0 p.m. which showed some one had got control over things. On waking up (it being Saturday morning) and having finished a late breakfast, we strolled round a bit, and then sat under an enormous flamboyant tree in full bloom to watch for the arrival of Alec and Rosenthal who should have been here last night; this was worrying for having only expected to be one night, we had sent our carriers off back to Wenchi at 7.30 a.m. and had hired a car to take us after midday. No sign of our friends, but the Omanhin came to call on us of which we we were extremely glad, and we welcomed him warmly. Osei Mensa, for that is his name, is the present head and representative of the Royal Family and was accompanied by his brother a fine young man who in the usual cloth and sandals, but with a mother-of-pearly wrist watch in a gilt chain, stood by him as he could talk English. There were as always a number of sword, stool and umbrella bearers accompanying them. The Chief made a handsome apology to David for not having the rest-house cleaned and the surround tidied up before we arrived, the reason being that the messenger sent from Ejura to inform him had only arrived this morning, which was quite true. So a pleasant little talk ensued, and we parted after taking a photograph and warm handshakes and smiles instead of an atmosphere of reproof which might have rather spoilt the first meeting of a Commissioner and his principal and most powerful Chief. After another wait of about an hour and still no Alec and his friend, we gave it up, climbed up into the hireling car which was a sort of wagonette and driven like a shooting star by an ex-Nigerian engine driver, we arrived back at Ejura shaken but safe somewhere around 2.30 p.m.; with us in our wagonette we had Moussa, Mensah (the Clerk), Ali, Bawi, three live fowls and some yams, the driver and one dog!

Sunday January 28th finds us now reasonably installed in our new home, but it wasn't so last night for the camp beds we had taken to Mampong never got back here at all; this was miraculously solved by D. unearthing an old camp bed in a wooden frame and some still good canvas lining which he had used in the forests in Burma for five years before 1912! On his first tour out here he had brought it with him, and kept it in reserve without using it until now. Altho' it was a single bed we managed somehow to sleep on it last night without discomfort—being such hot weather at the moment, it did not require much bedding nor we much clothing! The word clothing reminds me that Moussa suddenly asked David yesterday evening to take a shot at him if he put on a special armoured coat he'd bought at Wenchi before leaving there. He had been assured that the wearer would be immune from death by gunshots and just wanted to prove it. D. rather naturally wished to examine the coat which was a long well-made Hausa riding coat, the front and the back being covered with little squares of red leather or squares decorated with hyena, leopard, and lion skin, each containing a bit of writing from the Koran. We found Moussa very strong on this immunity and its reasons— also I think because he'd paid no less than £5 5s. for it, a lot of money in this country. After considerable thought D. got out of it by saying that the immunity only applied to a pagan Dane gun or a Fra-Fra arrow, that it was not intended to apply to good European weapons, and after being genuinely admired by us as a specially good coat the owner carried it proudly away. We went out to luncheon with Migeod at his delightful little house in the official bit nearer the village; it is L-shaped with a wide low verandah where we lunched in the cool, and is set back from the road in a pleasant clearing by itself. We hear that the cinematograph pictures are being done in Mampong today. In the afternoon we lazed on our own verandah, and had 'Evensong' in the open.

It is now the evening of the 31st January, David and I having spent the morning with the Zongo Chiefs and the Omanhin explaining and marking out the projected improvements to the whole village, a sort of face-lift which Ejura the land-port as it were for the Northern Territories, has long needed. With Mensah and the little Ashanti town clerk we had subordinates most anxious to set things moving and a modern slaughter house, a better market, and a larger and more secure cattle kraal were soon marked out and will be government constructed. For the drovers it is the *first* real touch they get with the markets since leaving Gambaga, Bole, Wa or even Nigeria; the motor car road being the final key.

On the way back I saw a large eagle (crested) tied to a stick in the ground and asked D. to buy it for me which he did for 1s. 9d. We then had it brought back with us to the house, where I put him on a rock by the verandah and personally gave him some pieces of meat that he accepted with dignity at the same time looking round at everything carefully. He appeared to accept me anyhow, but I think he had been so long tied up that his pinions wouldn't move properly and he remained where I put him until dark. Perhaps like myself he is waiting for a new month to start life again!

CHAPTER VIII

# The Famous N.T. Road

On this first day of February 1917 I was called as usual by
Mama but with the news that, while the eagle has gone, the
kitten given us by Migeod recently has re-appeared. It must
have been terrified by a thunderstorm and hid itself in the
round house we call the Martello Tower where there was an
old discarded mattress in the corner. So our verandah breakfast
on a lovely cool morning was shared with the kitten, some tame
pigeons, and our dog Hankuri all quite friendly to each other.
D's departure to the Court was soon followed by Tani, Fatima,
and Ajima to market with enamel basins on their heads while
Ali, the 'cordon bleu', followed majestically on his bicycle.
After a look round the garden and arranging for household jobs
with Mama, I hastened to get ready to receive a new guest in
the shape of Mr. Hertig a young Swiss-French cattle dealer
whom D. had met yesterday in the Zongo, and obviously not
very comfortable or even well-fed, all on his own. He had
recently arrived down with 298 cattle from North-West Nigeria.

He turned up about 11.15, and proved to be a delightful
guest and a very interesting one; luncheon not being till any
time after 12.30 we were able to have a real talk together. He
was working in a small cattle trading business of which the
head man who is some 40 years old has been 18 years in charge,
from the Niger downwards. Hertig himself had left Coomassie
on August 21st and only arrived back here from the H.Q. on
the Niger five months later, a few days ago; the present trade
is very poor owing to lack of money among both the Ashantis
and the Coast tribes and merchants, cocoa which normally
finances this part of the world having failed since war began

as a remunerative source. At one period he was within three days journey of Timbuctoo where the French had been having a poor time with their natives who aided by several thousand (exaggerated?) wild Touaregs (or Senussis?) had threatened a march on that city, which was militarily such an important base that all leave had been stopped until the danger subsided. He has disposed of 200 beasts here, but after the tremendous journey the rest are weakening daily, and two or three die frequently. They are the same handsome beasts that we saw at Wenchi, and very strong; Hertig said that they swim across the Niger as a start, and then all the way down are possible victims for lions, two or three of which he saw near Salaga eleven days ago—the previous one seen being actually on the Niger's bank! The driving is generally done by night as cooler and easier to keep moving, the drovers being practically always Fulanis, a tall light-coloured very gentle people, and just the type to do the long days and watchful job. At Waggadugu, the principal town in the Moshi country, there is a French Catholic priest who has been in the one place 17 years, and never wears a topee or a hat, having got quite immune to the sun's rays; I am inclined to think that the French stand these hot climates better than we do.

During the afternoon D. and I spent quite a time over the latest news from home in papers and letters, including a long list of New Year honours and Sir Douglas Haig's dispatch as to the war area. In the evening, when we wandered round the garden and compound, Ali suddenly produced a Fra-fra boy from far away up North whom David had known on a previous tour as the punkah boy at the W.A.F.F. mess in Coomassie. He is now on his way back there, his master, Captain Wheeler the Commissioner at Gambaga in the N.T., having died of yellow fever three months ago. He is rather a nice-looking boy with lines cicatrized on his face, but not so deep as to leave ugly marks. He spoke a little English and Hausa, but the Fra-fras themselves are still a savage race who romp about with bows and poisoned arrows; it is reckoned that they kill about one policeman a year in the Districts they inhabit. We got 'Bushmeat' as the boy was called to do us a bit of their famous dance on the verandah, which he readily acquiesced in, but to be really correct it should be done with no clothes on, so owing to my presence he was fitted out with a pair of shorts by Mama, and the game was on. Up and down he jumped hitting his chest alternately with his right and left knees, and then made a choking sound with his mouth and clapped his hands and beat his face and chest, finally stamping his feet, all in perfect time. Our boys watched and laughed their heads off; it must be great when done by a large number of his own tribesmen together.

During the night that followed we were both awoken after the moon had gone down by a strange noise quite close, a mixture of a roar and a low growl consisting of five notes— three ascending and two descending. We both lay without speaking, and heard this curious call repeated about five times. Then it stopped, and we asked each other what it could be; I promptly suggested a lion, and D. thought it might be, but lions are hardly ever seen or heard of as far South and usually remain the other side of the Volta. David had shot one near Kintampo in 1913, where he came on three, but that was very unusual, and it was a good deal West of Ejura as well as more North. After hearing the same noises again much further off we fell asleep. In the morning, as the prisoners led by a police-man were going down as usual to the water supply, D. told them to look out for tracks, and sure enough the policeman returned almost immediately to report a lioness and two cubs who must have crossed right through our pineapple grove near enough to have been seen, if it had still been bright moonlight. We and the boys all went off to see for ourselves, and there at one spot particularly was the clear imprint on wet sand of a full grown lioness and the smaller ones of the cubs with her. They had evidently come out of the bush across the road beneath us, come through the far end of the compound to the water, and then passed across to the East obviously making for the Afram plain, an uninhabited stretch of country many miles in width. I'd have given anything to see the adorable little cubs, and the mother too if she had waited to be looked at! The normal domestic morning alone, with D. away at the Court, felt duller than usual after this excitement, until two missionaries on motor bikes buzzed up about midday. One was a Canadian called Bamfield, quite talkative and had been in the Belgian Congo, Cameroons, and Nigeria—his fellow traveller was rather silent, and I didn't get his name. They left after a little refreshment, and D. returned to a late luncheon telling me that he had sent Moussa to Attabubu on the N.T. road to make preparations for us there when going through it on our tour fixed for next week.

During the next eight days we had quite a lot of bad news, both about the war—ships torpedoed, food getting scarce and general restrictions at home—and very much so also out here. Wenchi which we only left three weeks ago is to be closed, our successor Cutfield being moved to the N.T. where one of their men is ill, and another has to replace someone at the Secretariat; Juaso which David had early in his first tour is also being closed, and no leave, no resignations, no moves at all for the time being for anyone. Possible trouble in the N.T. necessitating some troops being sent up there will at any rate help D. to feel he is fully employed, and this with hurrying on the new lay-out and new building in the Zongo should keep us all flat out for a time. A good thing indeed as one doesn't have time to wish for other jobs in other places if hard at work. Migeod who is up and down a lot keeps us in touch with the world, and has become a real devoted friend to us.

We tried a new type of inspection one of these uninteresting days, and that was to go really early, just after dawn, and spend anything up to two hours at it *before* breakfast. It turned out to be a tremendous success, D. having notified this two days previously as he had thought it might be a flop otherwise. With Moussa treading delicately behind us we picked up Mensah, the head clerk and Osai the town clerk near the Court, while the Omanhin and the road overseer soon joined us at the main village entrance. Unlike some of the villages we had seen in the Western Province, Ejura is both picturesque and tropical; there are some very fine palm trees, beautiful and large mangoe trees covered with a pinky blossom, and many others of which I do not know the names. How I wish we had a book about the trees out here, and also the birds; every day I admire an unknown and still can't discover anybody to explain things. Before we got far with our inspection it was obvious that all the talks and plans made a week ago had already blossomed into facts, and it is quite extraordinary how in places the difference struck one. Burning piles of rubbish, sticks, old thatch from unoccupied houses combined with pits for bottles and other unwanted things had already tidied up a considerable area of the Ashanti village, and the start of the new Nkoranza road (which comes under the Omanhin) had at last made it look as if it really was a road and not a track one was lucky to find at all. Having disposed of the local village area of Ejura, we were soon hooked on to the Zongo Chiefs and their men who were all delighted to be able already to show the foundations and other necessary betterments such as drains for the new slaughterhouse site—and also a completely cleared new cattle kraal. Ejura is a place where sometimes far more animals have to be retained than could be cared for properly and it was a vital need to enlarge the capacity. We expect to find a similar problem at Attabubu.

The Zongo personnel here are good fellows, so polite; one or two of the horsemen turn out on these occasions, and accompany us round everywhere.

Back to breakfast at 8.45 after a good walk on a cool bright morning, and everyone we met seemed to be in the best of spirits. Ours soon sank however when after breakfast we were told that white ants had got into the store shed, and were doing all they could to devour stores and destory our clothes, of which there were quite a few boxes still unpacked. This meant all hands to the pump, and the rest of the morning was spent in opening up and emptying out, burning, flooding, disinfecting, and generally carrying death to the ants in every corner; the discovery was just made in time, so with luck we'll be all the better for it once it is (we hope) over. Being a Sunday (February 4th) the afternoon was quite a day of rest in two respects, and we held our little private service in the verandah just before tea. I have just finished H. G. Wells's 'Mr. Britling Sees it Through', which I enjoyed better than any book read recently; it is so obviously the view taken of the war in its initial stages by the average Briton.

February 11th. We started on our first tour today, which will take us in stages up to the river Pru which is the N.T. boundary; it can be best done by a thorough inspection on the way, so today we only covered about 6 miles to the first stopping place— Wirabon, a Zongo founded by old soldiers and boasting no rest-house as yet. It was really too hot (for we had started late) and I hammocked but David had bicycled on in order to have a native house prepared before our arrival. Even cleared out the small native houses are not too attractive for eating or sleeping in (this one had a colony of guinea pigs which were being evacuated at the moment I got there!), so we used the house to put loads and other bits and pieces in, ourselves eating and sleeping under a sort of temporary tent the boys contrived with two large green canvas sheets and poles borrowed from some of the Moshi carriers. But the 11th February will always be remembered by me as the night when I couldn't sleep properly for it was either too dark, or at times the moon was too bright, or insects beset me, or I had nightmares! I felt grossly unrefreshed in the grey light of the morning.

However, Amantin the next village, which was only 10 miles further along the road, soon revitalized my spirits for it has an excellent rest-house and offices quite near the village, and is a regular and favourite stopping place for everyone from the North. The Zongo Chief had met us on horseback near the river, with an escort of 4 pi-dogs, saluted, and galloped off back, while the Amantin village Chief, an Abrong, was talking with D. at the rest-house when I arrived. The village itself was clean beyond dreams and a very pretty place with not dust or untidiness whatever, but the Zongo which we looked at as well was being cleaned up and not really finished. It was however too hot at 10.30 a.m. to move about, and the boys having got things ship-shape in the rest-house we retired there before lunching and drank cool fresh lime drinks, and wallowed in baths, or shaved in D's case. He had hardly done this when some transport men who had been with the post as far as Yeji came in with a man whom they had caught smuggling gin, which is not allowed in the N.T. He was taking it to Prang the first village beyond the Pru, having come North from Coomassie. After we had lunch, D. heard the case and decided to send the man on to Prang while we kept the gin here and took it with us—the case could then be enquired into on the spot, for the accused says that he is slightly touched with leprosy and that the doctor at Prang had told him to go down to Coomassie, get some gin, and bring it back for medicine in his own town and under the doctor. Nothing much happened in the evening; we walked to some of the local farms on the chance of a guinea fowl or some other game, but no signs anywhere of them; we did however see quite near to us a full-feathered, quite lovely hoopoe with its crest erect and looking a regular prince among birds. The Court Clerk Mensah has been sent on to Akokoa, the next village, to get two hunters to meet us on the road tomorrow as it is a well-known game ground. We got up by lamplight at 5.30, and after a quick breakfast were soon on the road with Moussa and Bawi, leaving the others and the loads to follow slowly until they met us at the trysting place where we expect to find Mensah and the two hunters. It was going to be a very hot day, but at that hour it was like walking on a beautiful autumnal morning down a wide ride in a covert at home; the chief difference being that there were no high trees, and that a lot of the grassland had been burnt by forest fires. After about an hour we met the hunters, two small men in dirty one-piece costumes, carrying long Dane guns with primitive powder flasks and flints. David, having two rifles .577 and .318 with him, handed over the archaic weapons to me for forwarding to Akokoa when the carriers arrived; the hunting party then left, visible for some distance across a burnt area of ground with small leafless trees on it, while I with Bawi and Hankuri whining feverishly sat guard over the local armoury! The rest of our party soon arrived—Ali, Mama, Tani, and the carriers, plus the Ejura carpenter who, having no immediate job to do, had asked if he could come with us, never having seen the North Road before; I felt free to look around then and, walking about 100 yards followed by Mama with my 20-bore gun, I suddenly heard the long drawn out whistle of the green pigeon. Seizing the gun, and snapping two cartridges in correct story book fashion into the breech I spotted the three where they were and on nearing it fired too soon and missed one, but after a quick follow up I got one with my second shot to my delight. Shouts of 'Ya faddi' (it's fallen) from everyone, Mama varying it by 'Sanu aiki' (a good work, or congratulations on the work) —and it was picked—so we were certain of a nice bird for our dinner. We then travelled on to the village some 6 or 7 miles, where we were met by the linguist and soon settled into the rest-house; I found myself rather proudly giving orders as to send for wood and water, arrange earth closets, fix the Union Jack, and borrow a pestle and mortar for pounding fu-fu or other foodstuffs. On the way here I had suggested to Ali, Mama and Mensah (the Clerk) and the carpenter, who all had bicycles, that they could all go ahead and arrive here before me, but NO! not one of them would accept the chance, they were with me and had to look after me, and no one could persuade them that it was right to go unless I was with them. It was a happy touch, and made one reflect that these different seven or eight types of Africans are happy serving and travelling with white people who they instinctively know both trust and like them for themselves. It was a pretty little village, favoured by the many travellers from the North and well kept; the rest-house was only some two years old and was slightly away from the thatched and re-earth walled houses. D. arrived earlier than he had expected for the day was too hot and the ground too open, although he had seen plenty of tracks. After a quiet luncheon and rest we conferred with the linguist and ordered some windows to be made in the rest-house, and the thatched roof to be lowered all round and so prevent the rain from blowing in under the eaves. Soon there was a storm with the usual lightning and then rain; an early bed was gladly taken by everyone. Next morning D. got up even earlier, and left with the hunters at 4.30, hoping that the rain would have shown up tracks of game, and the bush fires of which there are some daily would have driven beasts in the direction the hunters were taking. But alas! it was again a blank day, although soon after the first dawn they had put up an oribi, a small antelope, but of course let it go for fear of warning bigger game, and then had been quite near to a good sized roan, but a female, which D. rightly also spared. The only product of their early start and keen searching for a proper quarry was an enormous 4 foot very fat puff-adder almost trodden on by one of the hunters! Our Moshi carriers had its skin off in no time, for they apparently enjoy the meat as a rare prize! A quiet evening was only enlivened by David's pleasure at finding a Valentine (it being February 14th) which I had drawn, written suitable wording below it while he was away hunting, and had then pinned it to his clean shirt which he would have to wear after his bath. It was poisonously hot, so again we undressed as soon as we could and entrusted ourselves to Morpheus.

Thursday, February 15th. We were called at a quarter to six

and were off by 6.30. Two Fulanis had walked over from Jatto
Zongo with news of an assault case, for which we got Tani to
interpret Moshi into Hausa for Moussa and David's benefit,
and as we were going that way we took the two men along with
us. D. and I walked together for about 2 hours, and then I got
into my hammock, but he took his bicycle and went on ahead
to commence hearing the case. Leaving him at Jatto for
rounding-up witnesses, I and the carriers pressed on towards
Attabubu, the headquarters of the Brong tribes, and for many
years famous in the history of this road to the North. From
there on the country became more and more open, and we
passed streams of people with loads and a whole crowd of
drovers with donkeys; one of them had got squashed into the
the middle of the road as he had no load on his back, and I
suddenly found myself in my hammock but resting on the
animal's back! He didn't kick or seem to object, and full of
laughter my boys carried on as if nothing had happened. Next
came a posse of women who all shouted 'Sanu, Mammy', 'Sanu,
Mammy' as we jogged past on the hot flesh-coloured road;
there were patches of green park-like country at times but
rather more burnt stretches, the recent storms having swept
the seasonal bush fires into the most odd corners, and completely
blasted dozens of the smaller trees. Nearing our destination we
met an enormous herd of cattle, dust rising round them in a
hazy cloud. One drover was an Arab, as D. (who was following
us) told me afterwards, which I was glad to know for he looked
lighter brown in colour even than the Fulanis whom one meets
more often than not. The sun got fiercer and fiercer, and the
travellers fewer and fewer, after eleven o'clock so that it was
with thankful hearts all of us entered the large rest-house
compound, which contains two main houses and five or six
smaller ones, with some wonderful mango trees and limes as
well as groups of Barbadoes pride and other flowering shrubs.
The mango trees are magnificent, like bell tents of dark thick
cool greenery. One can easily picture Dr. Montgomery living
here for nearly twelve months in 1900, when he was cut off
from Coomassie and the coast by the siege at the same time as
the little group of English officers at Kintampo had been in
considerable danger only protected by the Nkoranza Queen
Mother's influence. While the loads were coming in, the young

Omanhin, a very tall and beautifully proportioned handsome Abrong, came to pay his respects; D. was particularly glad to see him as we had planned to spend at least two, perhaps three, days here—hear cases, discuss new projects, and learn all that could be learnt about the trade passing up and down the road, and the tribal reaction to the war news.

After lunch we sat for some time under one of the largest mango trees and read books and papers until baths and a change were ready, after which in the comparative cool of five o'clock onwards we took a first stroll in the (to us) new town of our new District. At the outskirts of the Ashanti village, which is about ¼ mile from the rest-house, the Zongo people met us, two dear old Mallams on gaudily-bedecked barbs, velvet saddlecloths, jingling silver and coloured stuff bridles, all the mediaeval trappings that delight the eye. All the elder 'Sarikin Zongo' in dark blue robes and turbans came forward, with kola-dyed teeth and poached egg looking eyes, to shake hands with David—four of the Mallams were hadjis, having made the pilgrimage to Mecca; the dear old toothless fellow on horseback having been the first who had ever done it from here. They drew our attention to a crowd of smaller fry bearing bundles of yams and so forth as presents to us, and we 'na-godia'd' and 'sanu'd' and 'na gida'd' all round, and then passed on, while they went off to their Zongo half a mile further; the Ashantis had brought a sheep and other gifts. The village, being a very old one, had in the middle of its broad clean main street four or five of the most wonderful big ficus trees, thick dark green pinnacles of foliage about 100 foot higher or taller. There were actually two or three coconut palms also, and a banana grove, with a tremendous cotton tree and a parasite ficus growing on it. The huge cotton tree base looked like a gigantic elephant's foot grey and bloated. On one side of the trunk was a vast swarm of bees who have lived there from time immemorial, and help to drive away the enemy in battle!—They are said to fly out also if any wicked person passes close by! Then there was another interesting thing. Lying near a house inhabited by an old woman was a partly broken copper bowl with a beaten design on it. Popular supposition is that it fell from heaven once upon a time, but a former Commissioner named Rattray sent rubbings home to an expert who reported

that it was Moorish work of the 13th century, and that it had
on it an Arabic inscription meaning 'Allah is victorious'. How
it came here, however, is still a mystery, but it might well have
been a bowl used for eating and carried by a traveller from the
French Sahara side who had lost or thrown it away here during
his journey.

Next we proceeded to the Zongo which was a very large
widespread area with lots of delightful real north country round
houses, some in large compounds rather like farmhouses at
home. Cattle, guinea fowl, donkeys, hens, ducks, and many big
hound-looking tan-and-white dogs roamed freely around, and
all this outlined by the telegraph poles and wires running to
the northern towns—betokening a very different civilization.
As we came to the marker, it was nearly sundown and the final
buying or selling was being completed, the women sitting on
low stools with bowls of unknown contents in front of them,
or green leaves covered with red peppers, and calabashes of
rice. We had another talk with the Omanhin, and then decided
with him and Mensah (our clerk) as to meetings and cases
tomorrow, peeping in at his clerk's house, neat and business-
like, with pigeon holes containing pens and ink, a table with a
pink cloth on it and a large ledger, a Hausa grammar, and the
story of Robinson Crusoe—a glorious mixture!

Next day, February 16th, was even hotter than the last
scorching ones were, and as discussed last night the Court
proceedings were fixed for 8 o'clock under one of the largest
mango trees in our compound. While we were polishing off our
breakfast, we could see the people arriving and Mensah arranging the chair for D. in front of a table suitably set out with pen
and ink and books for reference. The Omanhin, his linguist,
and elders sat on their wooden leather-seated, gilt embossed,
chairs in a semi-circle in front of the table, others squatting on
the ground, and the Zongo representatives making a smaller
circle to complete the scene. Court began, and the voices
droned on in Hausa, Twi, and English when there was an
interruption to make known that a Doctor Le Fanu had left
Prang at 4 o'clock this morning and was arriving very soon.
I naturally would receive and look after him, so the Court
continued as before. The Doctor turned up soon after 9 o'clock
—a clever and nice looking elderly man wearing gold rimmed

spectacles and who was soon telling me about his trip and what he had been doing in the N.T. He is on the Agricultural side of the Government Service, and has been investigating the cattle plague deaths and causes at several of the villages and towns along the road from Gambaga southwards—but now completing his tour and thankful to get down to the Coast again at this time of year. We talked about the war, cattle, lions, and other N.T. experiences, for a bit and when his house was prepared for him I sent him across with books and papers galore to bathe, rest, and get ready for luncheon with us after midday; at that moment D's court was adjourned, a new and large mail arrived from home—which pleased everybody as it meant a quiet afternoon with papers and letters before the normal walk round between tea and the evening meal. Le Fanu was especially glad of this lucky meeting and rest, for he still has some way to go and had been all alone for nearly a week.

Next morning he was up at 3 o'clock, and one heard carriers moving, but we ourselves merely turned over in peace as we were going to rise late in view of another day here. We having dressed at leisure, and breakfasted under our big mango tree, got down to business soon after eight and embarked on a thorough inspection of the whole Zongo and market area with a view to planning and improving where possible. Guided by the vultures we investigated the present slaughter site first, a great stretch of ground with a bullock or two being cut up on it, not very attractive, nor healthy as too near one group of houses. The 'sarikin Zongo' and the 'sarikin fawa' (chief of the butchers) both agreed warmly on this, and a new area of ground further way was marked out and decided on there and then. Next we tackled the market where the people were bringing in their goods, and where the arrangement was not very good, for the meat stall was too near vegetables and clothes and odds and ends, especially as the trade is increasingly annually, and after the war will be greater still. So a butcher's shop was planned, and longer and bigger covered market stretches were proposed as for example at Wenchi. These ideas seemed to go down well at a palaver D. summoned under one of the trees just beyond the market end. After first discussing this town-planning scheme, D. spoke to the people about the war, and gave the mallams an illustrated paper written in

Arabic, and published by the Overseas Club. It was all pictures of ships, soldiers, guns, and other war happenings, and very well done. It was curious to see an Arab among the throng with a real olive face, a hooked nose, and a very black beard, and wearing a white turban wound round a red tarboosh. He held by the hand a dear little boy with a perfect little pale brown face and almost European features. The father came forward and said that the child had a very sore leg, and explained to D. in Hausa that he'd like to have a letter to a Doctor; this of course was easy, either Coomassie or Salaga, whichever the man would like best, and he chose Coomassie; it had been bad luck that this had not been known yesterday when Le Fanu could have treated it. This interruption over, D. explained the importance of a clean and healthy town, and thus of the slaughter needs and traffic wants, ending up by pegging out a new straight bit of road as approach to the market instead of the present uneven and dirty one. Our work done, we retreated to our tree-shaded compound, and amused ourselves with chess and papers until bedtime.

At last we felt on rising that this was to be an unusually happy day for from the moment we took the road at about 5 o'clock, we knew that our journey ended at the river Pru and the boundary between our District and the Northern Territories of which we had heard so much from Captain Armitage and other senior officers. As we stumbled our way through the dark, we heard hushed voices in the Ashanti village and a dog growling in the Zongo, otherwise the world was still asleep and full of early morning scents, stronger than usual after the night's rain. After a bit the moon came forth, and then below it the dawn showed faintly, and suddenly it was day. We met nobody until seven o'clock when a boy riding on a horse passed us who had come from Tamale, had been Captain Armitage's washerman, and was now going to Coomassie. Soon after that we saw hyena tracks, and a little later an awful coughing sound rent the air, which was a baboon some way off the road. It was really very pleasant walking in this early clean atmosphere, and I watched with appreciation some parrots flying over us, their grass-green plumage and orange red breasts lit up by the sun's rays. The grey and red kind inhabit the thicker forest rather than this open country. After walking about 3 hours I

said I'd hammock, and David went ahead on his bicycle to the
Pru river where Moussa had been dispatched the day before,
in order to arrange with the Zongo and other labour a camp
for us on our bank. During this next part of the journey there
was one small Zongo but no real village, and wide generally
flat open country with small trees and not much forest visible.
All of a sudden it seemed that we saw in front of us a steep yellow
bank on the top of which D. and Moussa were perched looking
at the river below them. The Pru, which runs North-East from
Nkoranza where we slept on our way from Wenchi, and joins
the Volta about 30 miles North of this ford, is about 40 yards
wide here with a flat smooth-stoned bottom and quite shallow
just now. It is lovely to look up and down its course, smooth
flowing and shaded by trees on the overhanging banks. Our
camp was nearly ready, and it all looked gay and exciting—
a marvellous change from forest country. As soon as I arrived
with the carriers close behind me, David disappeared with two
hunters of the Attabubu Omanhin's people, and the Prang
Chief from Prang, a village on the N.T. side, who had all been
told to take him and explore the country nearby so that they
could plan tomorrow for a private shoot. He came back after
only an hour away, and said the country must be chockfull of
game as he had seen plenty of tracks, and that the Prang Chief
had shot a kob but they hadn't succeeded in finding it. D. had
not taken a rifle with him as there was no time for a decent
day at it once the morning hours had gone.

Apparently less than 3 miles upstream there are one or two
hippopotami, and any where there might be a crocodile, so for
the first time I have found myself in the Africa that one always
heard of as a child. Added to that, or because of that, I crossed
with Moussa to the other side of the river and suddenly put up
a great number of guinea fowl of which (though missing the
first barrel) I secured a nice fat one with my second shot. This
unexpected contribution to the larder was soon surpassed, as
about an hour later David who hadn't been able to resist a
short walk upstream with the hunters on the Ashanti side came
back with a fine young kob he had shot not more than 500 yards
from the crossing. Everyone was delighted, and songs and bathing engaged the hammock boys until darkness prevented
further amusements. There were plenty of other birds about

among which I watched a small grey heron sitting on a rock in the river, had a quick view of a pair of black and white birds rather like small kingfishers as to size and flight, and then spotted another beautiful little bronze-coloured bird perched on a branch over the river bank. After supper, and a little service read to the music of the lapping water, we sat in front of our tent while bush fires lit up the sky in one direction, great bull frogs started a raucous deep-throated croaking almost outdoing the thunder which continuously reminded us of its presence, and up through a break in the trees we caught sight of Orion's Belt and one or two other stars before going to sleep under our mosquito nets. Next morning D. got up at skreich o' day and pushed off with the hunters, but I took it easy and breakfasted by the river about 7.30, while the hammock boys and carriers were rigging up odd tables for plates and crockery to be laid on, also steps in the sand banks above the river. After that I watched the continuous activity at the ford, women washing calabashes or babies, donkeys crossing, a fisherman like a bronze statue casting with a graceful sweep of his arm while wading up and down; the Chief had sent him out to get some fish for us as they are good eating here, and often quite good sport. D. returned radiating heat after a blank morning, and we both removed most of our clothing and lay on some flat stones in the river below the crossing for about an hour; it was marvellously cool. In the evening Moussa and I went to see some recent elephant tracks about $\frac{1}{2}$ mile below the crossing and on our return to the ford met a man with a bow and arrows as well as a spear; it looked delightfully primitive. D. had another blank hunt, largely because he was actually stalking a fine group of kob and trying to pick out a good head when a gang of Dagarti carriers passed near the ford shouting and singing, which scared the beasts off in a gallop. During dinner, it being dark of course by then, we heard weird sounds coming up from the river bed below us, rather like a drowning man groaning at his last gasp. Ali said it was a crocodile, and we heard it three or four times—I tried to see it lit up by flashes of lightning but no luck. It rained in the night, which would help the hunters as we can only spend two more whole days here, and probably will not get a chance of coming up again for a long time.

The 'white hunter' and his companions were again away before I arose, and the ford was rather busier today, more animals crossing (a Fulani trying to urge four donkeys to cross together had a rotten time before, oh! how patiently, he succeeded), and the Chief's fisherman casting again while two large fish were being cleaned for him by a carrier. From Prang, a boy arrived with a present of two pineapples for us, and soon after him a 'post-to-post' man with a basket of vegetables from Migeod. I heard that David was on his way in, having had a kill, so went out to try and meet him; as it happened, when I did come across him, he was trying to stalk and kill a crocodile but was just too late for a shot before the creature dived. He had, however, secured a really good kob with a fine head, the hunters arriving in camp bearing it just after we ourselves had returned. Mama and the bailiff were sent off to Ejura yesterday, Mama to get some more stores and clothes, and the bailiff to post letters and return with another mail; they both have bicycles so will probably be back this evening. As it happened, a mail did arrive here after luncheon today, but not so welcome as usual for it brought news of D's father having died of pneumonia in London during February. He had been doing King's Messenger to Russia, and fell ill while sleighing round the Gulf of Finland, lay up in Stocholm for a bit, and then became worse and passed out in London soon after arrival there. We were both so fond of him, and it has made us very unhappy, but one can't do anything at this distance so must just carry on in the ordinary way. We decided to take an evening walk in the game country and soon put up a small oribi, two kob but not within certain shot, and some hartebeeste. We came back along the river bank in a stretch of slow sluggish brown water rather suggesting de Vere Stacpoole's 'The Pool of Silence'. One could imagine it full of crocodiles with gaping maws, and I did see tracks of a hippopotamus on the bank close by. The following morning D. got a distant view of three waterbuck of which two were bulls, fighting presumably for the girl; however they could definitely not be stalked over an open flat plain of about 900 yards, so had to be left to themselves. He was grubby enough anyhow when he did return as there had to be a good deal of stalking on burnt ground for, the small trees being as a rule also burnt and blasted, there was little if any cover to conceal one. During the afternoon a huge herd of the strong humped cattle came from the North, 165 in all; it was good to see the way the poor beasts rushed down the steep banks, raising a cloud of yellow dust, and rejoiced in the water after a long hot march. Water is very scarce at this time of year, and the Volta, the Pru, and the Afram are the only large rivers on the way from the N.T. to Coomassie. Today for the first time I saw a goodly company of Tuaregs, who are the most picturesque and fierce-looking of all the races one sees here.

They look like a mixture between Fulani and Arab, tall, slender and brown; their sinister impression is heightened by the dark blue or white veils they wear over their mouths and noses, sometimes over their eyes also. They wear blue and white clothes and carry spears—a group of them look like the popular idea of a dervish; indeed I believe that in their own country round about Timbuctoo and the desert they are both fierce and lawless. An old man who was having a rest sitting down with his face uncovered was much amused by my jumping down a steep bank on to the sand of the road, and imparted this illuminating action on my part with great gusto to a young man who was busy with his load; his mouth was covered, but his eyes and nose gave the impression of a good-looking, slender fellow, as graceful as a deer. I was awfully pleased to see a 'time bird' flying up the river, a gorgeous and brilliant blue body with a red comb. Mensah who was with me said they tell the time, calling at 6, 7, and so on throughout the day. Further down there was a large bird resembling our cormorant diving for fish, and then gorging himself with his catch on a rock. The old crocodile was groaning again last night, and we called Ali to go with a lantern to investigate, but before he got to the water's edge there was a splash as it floundered off the bank into the river. Moussa had been lent David's rifle for a treat during the afternoon and never bagged anything, but had the luck to find a good kob close to the place where D. had shot at and though he'd failed to hit it this morning. The hunters had passed within 10 yards of where it was found, and said it must have run just out of sight and dropped stone dead. This one had a better head then the previous one, so D. is quite satisfied with the result of this hunting holiday, having secured 5 kob, two of them nice trophies; he says he must have seen as many as 150 in the three days, which rather accounts for the comparative scarcity of the other beasts he had hoped to get—the river had evidently a special attraction for this lot. From dinner onwards everyone was busy dismantling the camp, packing up, and calling the carriers and hammock boys in from Prang on the N.T. side in anticipation of an extra early start tomorrow when we leave for Ejura again, and have to arrive at Attabubu early in order to continue a case already half heard.

Almost as soon as we woke up, and had consumed some breakfast, David with Mensah the clerk disappeared in the misty dawn on their bicycles so as to get on with the case at Attabubu before the midday heat. The servants and I did not hurry as it was only $2\frac{1}{2}$ hours or less that we had to cover, and I walked almost all the way until Moussa and the carpenter made it quite clear to me that it would look better if I entered the village in my hammock! Actually I was not loth to do that, for the sun rose quickly and except for a period when there were some enormous anthills, brown and high with pinnacles like miniature cathedrals, there was nothing to see that I hadn't met before. I got into the hammock and buried myself in an old 'Times', while the hammock boys soon recovered their old stride and we sped grandly past the Zongo and the village, to arrive in the big rest-house compound where David was holding full Court under the shade of a big mango tree, surrounded by what looked like remnants from a jumble sale! This was the second part of the debt case heard first on our way up, in which a man from Akokoa had claimed half the estate of the last Omanhin of Attabubu who had died a year or more ago; he alleged that at no time had anything like his share reached him, and that the missing share was all tucked away in other people's keeping or pockets here. There were bags of money, gold dust, cloths, a chair ('stool') or two, a pair of sandals, a few pieces of rough jewellery, and an elephant's foot, all arranged before David for division. I'd never seen gold dust before; it looks like very fine shore gravel. By midday the case was successfully accomplished, and soon after, with all the boys and the baggage having arrived, we sat down to lunch and welcomed the afternoon rest. Later I watched Bawi knocking limes off one of the trees in the compound, and then had to rush inside the verandah when a crashing storm with cool, heavy rain completely deadened other sounds and stopped all work for $\frac{3}{4}$ hour; ten minutes later it was just a beautiful bright evening, and D. summoned another Court which was quickly staged in the compound as before. There were only two cases, but one was a criminal one, and concerned a man from Wa in the N.T.

The man in question had stolen a fish from a small boy, and when the father remonstrated, Ali from Wa had let him have it with a knife in his hand. There were a few cuts, none serious, but the motives were hardly good and, the evidence being strongly corroborated, D. awarded him imprisonment for six months. He was a hefty looking fellow and a bad hat to judge by his appearance; consequently he was taken along to the town for safe keeping, and is to travel with us tomorrow for his imprisonment at Ejura. Soon after this the thunder and lightning began again, and made me wonder whether they keep a permanent Government storm here; it actually made one blink to be in such a dazzling atmosphere of blue, purple and white light. It went on from 8 to 10, and maybe after that, but there was a lull then, and we went to sleep. Next day we were up at 4.0 and walked across the compound to a hut in which breakfast was ready for us. All the staff having assembled and put on to packing, etc., David and I, proceeded by Poiga (a transport boy) with a lantern, led the way with Moussa and the prisoner who had a pair of handcuffs (locked), one being on his right hand while he carried a load of potatoes in a bucket with the free left hand. As the stars got paler a faint light appeared in the East and we dispensed with Poiga and his lantern since it rather spoilt the illusion and beauty of the early dawn, with the trees standing black against the clear sky. Suddenly there was a crash and a shout, and I turned round to see the prisoner making off into the bush, the grass at the side having now grown to a considerable height! Half a dozen boys and Moussa gave chase at once, and D. shouted to M., who had a rifle, to fire a warning shot, although the man was some distances away by then and we on the road could still just see him in the pale grey light. But it was no good. D. blew his whistle and the followers returned rather crestfallen, though they couldn't see over or through the long grass while they were chasing him; we had sent Chinsi up a tree, but that was no use either. The man had made his dash at exactly the right moment, had pretended to trip on the road, had dropped his bucket (Moussa turning round to see what had happened), and was away at once. The carpenter was sent back to Attabubu on his bicycle to warn the Omanhin and the Zongo Chiefs that a wide search should be made, and the Northern posts also warned; it would be difficult for the man to free himself from the locked handcuffs.

After this we walked most of the way to Jatto Zongo through rather copse-like country with (as the sun got higher) a whitish mist over some marshes which lay in the hollows; from the Zongo D. bicycled on to Akokoa to tell them the result of the case heard yesterday while I took the hammock again, and (after seeing another lot of Tuaregs) arrived also at Akokoa where we arranged to lunch, rest a little, and then go through to Amantin, the last rest-house before Ejura. We had hardly left Akokoa by more than 500 yards when D's back tyre went completely flat which, Mama having gone forward on his bicycle with the only pump, meant that he would have to walk all the way. Biga was sent on to recover the pump, while I went ahead in my hammock. Very soon I met a man with a bicycle on which my basilisk eye discerned a pump. What is more, the man was one of Captain Armitage's boys, and in fact was the one Captain Armitage had with him in Jermyn Street while on leave last year, and had served the tea to us on our visit to him in his rooms there! After that, all was well; but what a coincidence for it was exactly a year ago, Saturday February 24th.

After a good sleep in the nice little village of Amantin, we did a hard fast march all the way, 19 miles, to Ejura where we are now again at home, and eager to inspect every corner of our house, the garden, the pineapple grove, and to see what changes, if any, there were. The boys had arrived ahead of us, and luncheon was ready—after which we had a far too short call from a Mr. and Mrs. Bland (he is the Manager of the railway and lives in Seccondee) who had only recently been transferred from Nigeria, and were out just for the drive from Coomassie. They were delightful people, but had to go back early so we couldn't entertain them as we would have liked to do.

# CHAPTER IX

# Recruiting for East Africa

Nothing interesting seems to have happened since we returned from the camp on the N.T. boundary, though D. has had quite a few Court cases to deal with, and has been able to accelerate the town improvements. This morning however Mr. Migeod's deputy, named Haltermann, arrived up bringing a Mrs. Morris and a Captain Baker who were just sightseeing for the day from Coomassie. Later on D. returned from his office with Captain Dale Glossop and Mr. Johnstone who had marched in from Amantin this morning with a force of N.T. police on their way to Coomassie. They lunched with us, and as Mr. Johnstone had his pipes with him he gave us and all the servants a delightful half hour, walking up and down the verandah in the jaunty way of the real piper, and the lift of the right elbow which coaxes the tune out of the chanter. 'Lord Lovat's Lament', 'Portree Men', 'The Lochanside', 'Culloden Day', 'The Barren Rocks of Aden', and 'Highland Laddie' took us and our hearts back to the heather hills of Scotland. The two officers left by car for Coomassie later, followed by the police and some reservists in single file who were all going to camp further down the road for the night, and then next day on to Mampon.

During luncheon Johnstone, who had only come recently from home to Togoland and up from there to join Dale Glossop at Tamale in the N.T., told us a great deal about the voyage and the conditions now at sea. The 'Moewe' is now in the Atlantic again and is with submarines causing havoc in the area between America and the North African Coast, but the 'Abinsi' in which Johnstone travelled had after 25 days at sea arrived all right, only being challenged by one of our own 'mystery ships' off Sierra Leone. It was at that port that he had learnt of the amazing story regarding some Australian Transports bound for England via The Cape. While on shore at Freetown some of the men saw an hotel with a German name, and promptly burnt it down, and another one as well, and worse than that one of the party being elbowed off the pavement by an African hit him so hard that the poor chap never recovered from it. Naturally an immediate enquiry was held on board the Anzac's ship and the punishment decided on was that no shore leave of any kind would be allowed when the squadron reached Dakar, its next port of call. In due course when they arrived at Dakar (although as a precaution the officer commanding had ordered a parade on deck in full kit while entering the harbour) about 2,000 of the men, once the ships had anchored, jumped off the ships simultaneously and were seen by the amazed citizens of Dakar swimming strongly to the shore and asserting their sights to land, rifles and uniforms being no hindrance. Even if there are sharks in the harbour, which I doubt, this invasion would probably have frightened them back to the sea for good.

Today, seven months exactly from our landing at Seccondee, was one full of visitors in all directions—Public Works, Agriculture (Mr. Evans especially interesting to me for advice on the garden), Veterinary, and Transport. It culminated in David taking the chance of a lift both ways and deciding to dash down to Coomassie for the night. He has been very worried by getting no answer from the C.C. to his request for leave home in order to settle his father's affairs, and arrange something for his mother who will now be all alone; I quite agreed with him, and was not at all worried about being left alone for the night even if it is for the first time in the 'bush'—the conditions here at Ejura are not comparable with a desert island, and our staff invariably rise to the occasion when it is something new. So after luncheon, about 2.30 p.m., Hankuri and I and the whole household from Moussa to Bawi watched and waved to D. from the Eagle's eyrie as Haltermann's car slipped away down the red road to Mampon and civilization. I thinned out some sunflowers and then gave tea to the Government Entomologist, a Mr. Simpson, who had been twenty-two months without home leave and looks pretty tired out; his travels have been quite amazing, Togoland, Nigeria, the Gambia, and Gold Coast—collecting information as to the effect that insects have on wild animals and birds in their natural surroundings. I think it was especially concerned with the tsetse fly. He is staying at the rest-house for four nights before going on in order to feel strong enough for the journey down to the Coast. It was a very solitary dinner that I sat down to, but before going to bed I was informed by the servants that (1) Mama and Tani are going to sleep in D's dressing room so as to be near me, (2) Moussa was to sleep on the verandah outside D's room and mine, and (3) that the Corporal (although *not* ordered to do so by D.) was to be patrolling the whole compound at night until dawn. Ali in his own hut was of course equally on the look out, as were odd hammock men and carriers —passim!—it sounds like an internment camp! During a bad thunderstorm about midnight, Mama came in with a lantern asking me if I'd like him to 'sit down small' while the storm continued!

Monday March 5th brought David back in Haltermann's car and they joined Simpson and myself at luncheon. D. had managed to get a satisfactory interview with the C.C. although any leave is probably impossible now the Moëwe is out again. We have had a letter from our nice hardworking clerk at Wenchi lamenting the closure of the post, and quite miserable about his transfer to Sunyani—one sentence ran 'As a matter of fact Sir since you left me, I have never been happy and don't feel lively. I am not sick but only discontent owing to loss of your worship and Mrs.' He was a first class clerk, and entered into everything, travelling, Court work, town inspections, even football with the hammock men; he deserves a really good post and an interesting one, unlike the average Coast born who dislike the 'bush'. Both D. and I do a good deal of Hausa together nowadays as he will have an exam soon for promotion to 'Higher Standard' classification, and I find it most valuable with the staff, as also Moshi which is simpler and only occasion-ally required. In the evenings a garden walk generally precedes this 'school hour' unless D. rushes off with a gun to kill a red-legged partridge as he did this evening. The thunderstorms and rains are almost continuous these days, and we really were very lucky in our Wenchi days—here the District is more static, there being few villages of any importance not served by the road—and crossing rivers and dry village houses for a temporary camp are hardly necessary. We had to send Simpson back to the rest-house this evening with a lantern and special hammock boys as the rain made it difficult even to go that short distance, perhaps $\frac{3}{4}$ mile. D. having gone with him I resumed reading French aloud out of 'Lettres de mon Moulin' which (aloud, I mean) is the best way of keeping up a language if one is alone —but it would sound odd if anyone came in unobserved!

Next morning I heard David getting up just before dawn, and was told when arising myself that he had gone down the road with Moussa into the newly grassed bit of the burnt country we saw from the verandah, on the cahnce of a shot at 'meat'! And it was so, for about 8 a.m. he walked in looking as if he'd seen nothing when quite suddenly, 'Oh! by the way, I got rather a nice hartebeeste down there', pointing to the bush country the other side of the road! Great joy, Nubila and another carrier having gone out to meet Moussa—and Mama, Ali and the rest beaming in anticipation of gorging the prize. Apparently he and Moussa had not gone very far in, perhaps a mile only from the road, when they espied a small herd of hartebeeste of which D. picked out the best one he could see properly (it was still the very early dawn) and fortunately bowled her over in one shot. The hartebeeste family both have horns, and this was a big female, but he'd naturally rather have got one of the males if possible. The meat is a bit strong for Europeans, but the skin is useful when dried, and the horns in this case were quite a good pair although slightly smaller than a similar male would have been. In the evening we got a green pigeon for our dinner, and before coming indoors we inspected the boys' houses—one Ali and his wife, another Tani and Mama, and the third Moussa and Asetu, rBawi sleeps in Tani's house too). They all have a medley of personal property, Moussa for example has seven fez's strung on a long line. Tani and Fatima were cooking hartebeeste meat, and Ali watched by his parrot was busy on our dinner.

March 8th, Thursday. A new mail in today, and three large boxes containing some of our clothes and other gear we had left in store at Coomassie last August before starting to Wenchi;

these were gladly welcomed as they had to be unpacked, and aired, and sorted, and generally looked through. We had almost forgotten about them. The news by post was not good, for all leave is completely banned owing to the new Admiralty orders which for the time being prohibit passengers in Elder Dempster ships on this West African run, the reason quite properly being the teriffic drive the Germans are making at this part of the Atlantic. Our spirits temporarily clouded by this news were livened up again by the rapture of the boys over the unpacking of the three boxes. They were in quite a bad way, the whole back of one box (luckily it had a tin interior) having been eaten by ants, the insides of others rather desecrated by ants also, and other insects, and moulded by green stuff; but inside were a lot of good clean clothes for both of us which only required fresh air and drying, and most of all welcomed was a hat box of mine with several real home hats inside. By the time we had finished unpacking and sorting the contents of all the boxes, the place looked like one of Selfridge's bargain sales! The next four or five days have been just ordinary H.Q. routine ones— D. at the Court every morning, I busy in and round the house and garden, and then in the afternoon both trying to keep reasonably cool in the house, David swotting Hausa for his exam while I tried to do some fancy sewing in order to repair damage to clothes evacuated from the boxes they had lain in for eight months. One day in the early cool 8.30-10.30 period we again did a sudden descent on the Zongo to see how the new schemes were progressing, and, followed by a number of the older men in their blue and white robes, and their sandals going slop-slop, shuffle-shuffle, behind us, were glad to be able to congratulate everyone on the work done. D. taking nothing for granted surprised them by leaning against the fence at the furthest part of the new cattle kraal to see whether it stood up; but all was well. Before returning to the house we spotted some reddish skins hanging up in the market, which on examination we found were good, soft leather very suitable for binding books; Captain Armitage had told us to look out for them, he having taken a goodish number home and used them to bind his books there. They weren't all that cheap, and we failed at first to secure them even in a prolonged bid and refusal exercise— the merchant wanted 3s. for little ones, and 6s. when bigger.

We went away, and when out of sight sent Moussa back with 8s. 6d. for the lot, a move that succeeded, and we took them triumphantly home.

Today, March 14th, we are back at Mampon, having left Ejura soon after 2 p.m. in the big Transport lorry on one of the hottest days we have yet had anywhere. The lorry (a Scot like ourselves—an Albion from Scotstoun) takes 28 loads, each person counting as 2 loads, and as we are going well equipped in order to do some visiting in that part of the District, we with servants and kit just about fill it nicely. Once packed in on the front seat of the lorry the wild pace our driver seemed to revel in had a cooling effect on us, and apart from a few minutes stop on the road to have a talk with Migeod who was on his way up there were no incidents; at Mampon we were greeted formally this time by the Omanhin in full kit, the Zongo Chiefs, and the ever-ready crowd that joins in on these occasions. They formed a semi-circle opposite the rest-house door, the Omanhin under a particularly gorgeous yellow and red umbrella with a silver fringe, the elders with gold-topped emblems held between their knees squatting at his feet, while the Queen Mother was near at hand, and the Prime Minister wearing an unusually heavy silver chain of office standing alongside his Chief. Osei Mensah himself had been the Chief of Bantama and keeper of the Royal Mausoleum there in 1900, and after that had succeeded to Mampon as being the nearest suitable member of the traditionally Royal House. (Bantama had been burnt down and utterly destroyed by the war.) He is a tall man of about 60, of commanding presence, a beard and a very knowing and intelligent eye. After the usual courteous preliminaries, David knowing that there were some difficult rocks ahead owing to a rumour of conscription for the war made an apt little speech of warm appreciation of Mampon and its people, thanked everyone for calling on him, and explained his programme as to visits round the District while remaining in the rest-house here. We find it much cooler here than at Ejura, and I believe this ridge of hills is in fact about 1,200 feet high, Mampon itself being pretty well on the top.

Next day, after a perfect sleep, it was quite grey and windy until the sun came through. For D. it was a full working day as first of all he walked with Mensah to Nsuta, a village 6 miles

away, there and back in the morning, and after luncheon had
a long spell of Court cases which did not release him until
almost sunset. Meanwhile I read, and wrote, and finally took
Mama with me for a sort of 'old ladies constitutional' on the
road instead of accompanying David and Moussa to the Zongos
as had originally been intended. The nearer one gets to civilization, the more the cases, even when there are no lawyers around.
Up to now, Ashanti and the N.T. being ruled rather as protec-
torates, lawyers have not been allowed to practise here and
have not been required; cases of importance in either of the
territories being allowed to appeal to the Courts in the Coast
if they are applied for. On Friday 16th we left at 9.30 a.m. for
Afiduasi, a biggish village about 31 miles from here and part
of the Mampon lands below the scarp.—We had to hire a car
from Coomassie to do this, but it was a lovely drive and well
worth doing; Mensah and the driver were in front, a Union
Jack in the bows, and Moussa, Mama, D. and myself behind—
I took a luncheon basket and a few papers for the midday rest.
All this area around Coomassie is full of war history and war
memories—the place we were going to had a connection with
Jabin where there was a good deal of fighting in Sir Garnet
W's campaign, and whose people were always, right down to
1900, rather cool in friendship with Coomassie. The road after
5 miles from Mampon descends the scarp by a network of
curves, and is as beautiful as it is terrifying when or if the driver
is a speed-fiend as ours was. On one side there was a rocky hill,
and on the other an ocean of tree tops below us, besides glimpses
of other forests and wooded hills; once at the bottom there were
farms, one being a Government experimental one, and a few
small villages and forest huts. At Jamasi a new Chief was waiting
to greet us, a very thin old grey-headed and grey-bearded
fellow, unearthed out of the bush somewhere South of Coomassie to succeed the previous one who had died, with no
obvious heir, and no Queen Mother available to find or choose
one. This resulted in a wrong man being put on the stool, who
had to be de-stooled when this man was eventually discovered
by one of the expert tribal genealogists. We stopped, D. shook
his hand warmly, the children piped up 'God Save the King',
a brass band played and competed with three or four Ashanti
drums—and on we went. This is mostly cocoa country, the

price today being 5s. a load instead of 45s. which it was when D. was near here in 1913, Afiduasi having then been in his District of Juaso; it is changed now to the Mampon area. After luncheon, having arrived at Afiduasi first, we inspected the police station, and then D. held Court outside. On the way back we passed Aguna, and, petrol giving out twice while ascending the scarp, we both got two brisk walks to balance our rather tiring and rocking car journey. At just on 5.30 we entered this Mampon rest-house again, and Hankuri, who had been washed in our absence, lifted up his voice and wept on beholding his beloved master and mistress.

St. Patrick's Day, March 17th. Having been unable to visit the Zongo or even the outskirts of the town so far, we leapt up at 6.30 and were out with Moussa before breakfast, all round the backs of the houses, and through the Ashanti town to the Zongos where we saw the familiar robed Northerners and their cattle which by the time they reach here are not so plump or healthy looking as they are at Wenchi or Attabubu. The Ashanti town was very clean and tidy, but the Zongos a bit under average and so merited a slight reproof. It was a sunny and breezy morning and we enjoyed the long tour we had made, getting back to our breakfast a little after 8 o'clock. It was soon obvious that we would not be able to start back to Ejura today as we had hoped to do, for the Omanhin and his sub-Chiefs came in full strength to the compound in front of the rest-house at about 9 o'clock, while at the same time Migeod sent up a note from Coomassie saying he would not be able to let us have a car today, or even perhaps tomorrow. Soon the long line of Ashantis formed up on the ground opposite the rest-house steps in front of which a table and chair were placed for David, with the Union Jack behind him, Mensah and Moussa standing on either side. It was noticeable that there were no representatives of the Zongos present. D. opened the proceedings by informing the Omanhin (as usual this is never direct on official occasions, and is done through the linguists on both sides) that they knew there was to be a 'war meeting' in Coomassie next week when each big Chief in the country had been asked to attend or to send a representative, and that the object of it was to suggest recruits, both for service in the field and for carriers with the W.A.F.F. in the East African campaign. This, D. said, was *not* enforced recruitment as rumour appears to have suggested, it was an appeal to the loyalty of the Nation which had carried on ever since August 1914 to work and produce cocoa, ground-nuts, other foodstuffs, and assist England in this defence of the world against the Germans who were trying to capture all countries, black or white, that could be of value to them. How much help would be given? From the very start it was clear that trouble was brewing, and there were audible shouts and grumbling even before the two speeches (D. to the Omanhin and the Omanhin to D.) had been translated and digested. Just as the meeting was breaking up a detachment of troops in cars, under the command of Captain Dale Glossop, passed on the road beside the compound and Migeod who was accompanying them came in to tell me that they were off to Bole where a rising was expected. The people there thought if we conscripted them the French on their border would cease to be Allies, and they at Bole would be lost; the Governor there-fore had decided to make this quick show of force before any-thing could happen. D. was at that moment suggesting that the palaver should be adjourned till tomorrow, which was agreed on, though with some reluctance and low murmurs of non-agreement. The Ashantis having all departed, David wrote a hurried not to Fuller (the C.C.) at Coomassie asking for him to send back by early morning something that he (D.) could read out at tomorrow's meeting pledging the Government to no enforced recruitment of anyone for any work whatever, but volunteers very warmly welcomed. So everything for the moment being at a standstill, we lunched, read papers, played patience and chess, and went to bed quite tired out after the early morning start.

During the night first one, and after a time another, drum began beating somewhere in the hills nearby, followed for about $\frac{1}{2}$ hour soon after midnight by the rumbles of several more. Sleep then took hold of us again, and we woke in due course to a fairly fine morning, and a jolly good breakfast of paw-paw with limes, eggs and bacon, and coffee at 8 o'clock. Soon after breakfast D. was looking at a 'Times' which had come by the last mail, and saw something about the Germans poisoning wells in Belgium to prevent people getting fresh water, reported but not verified. At that moment the Omanhin and his followers had all just settled down in the compound as before, but to the tune of at least two, or perhaps three, times the number of those present yesterday and also a great display of arms of all sorts. It was, of course, the result of the drumming we had heard at night; and in the first ten minutes by question and answer it was clearly said that 'if any recruiting was enforced, it would be resisted by force'—the war was not their affair, and was not going to be. David asked what did they know about the Germans—did they think the Germans were good people?—There was shaking of heads and the linguist said 'We don't know them'.—This was D's cue, and he read slowly for Mensah to be able to interpret very simply the report as to Germans poisoning wells, and that therefore they must be bad people whom we all want to fight. There was a silence, and then the Omanhin asked the linguist to repeat this news again, which he did. 'Then', said the Omanhin, 'we are ready to provide a few recruits or carriers to help you, because in our war with you sixteen years ago, we allowed your people in the Fort to go and collect water from the well outside every day for half an hour—we do not fight those who have not water for themselves.' A roar of agreement followed this pronouncement, and the palaver ended, David shaking the Omanhin's hand warmly and telling him that he would ask the Governor to recognise publicly the Mampon's loyal decision. Just after midday we managed to get a lorry up to Ejura, meeting on the way many of the military cars we had seen going up yesterday; the troops of course had marched on. Before leaving, D. wrote a note to Slater who was acting Governor (but purely and personally to him) that he might do well to come up and himself congratulate Mampon on his behaviour. We arrived back at our home before luncheon, and were not sorry to get back into quieter surroundings.

Next day news came from Coomassie that another 300 men were going to be sent to Bole; this meant a pretty quick hustle in village, Zongos, police barracks, and on the road, for carriers had to be found and recruited, a camp made ready, and warning given to the market *and* to other places on the way from here to the North. Within 24 hours the troops began arriving by car, officered by Captain Baker, Mr. Johnstone with his pipes, three white colour sergeants, Dr. Lorena, a telegraphist, and I believe another subaltern; but the stop at Ejura was not long, so that after an early luncheon the whole column was on the march before 2 p.m.—and a pretty hot march it would be. Migeod was up that evening and was able at dinner to give us some interesting news from the front, particularly good from Mesopotamia where we have taken Baghdad and are in apparent control of the country South of the capital. On March 26th we saw a new clerk called Nortye for the first time; he is taking the place of Mensah who had been working for seven years and thoroughly deserved proper leave. 'Naughty' as he is naturally called is, like Mensah, a Fanti from the Coast, the race down there being much the best for office and responsible work owing to their centuries of contact with Europeans in trade at every port. He seems to be a very nice little man, but has no Hausa which means that the Court and the District are lucky in D's presence here, for he will have to handle cases in that language just as Nortye would do in Twi, the Ashanti one, which is to a European considerably more difficult to assimilate. Migeod being away in connection with the Bole expedition, David is temporarily doctoring the carriers on his behalf, and finds it interesting even amusing at times although there is an enormous amount of malingering— the diseases they claim to have being generally invisible ones such as toothache, backache, lumbago and so on; out of eight cases one morning there were only two genuine ones. Dr. Dugon passing through from Salaga to Coomassie the other day happened to have five men claiming lumbago, so told them to drop their clothes; he then examined them all naked and when he had dealt with the last one he said 'All right, you can carry on now', upon which they all stooped down with the utmost ease, proving that they had quite certainly not got lumbago!

Learning from some source that Slater, the acting Governor, was somewhere in the neighbourhood, D. was very anxious to see him, and fortunately decided early on the morning of March 27th to accept a spare seat in a car going to Mampon and left here at 7 a.m. to see for himself. I busied myself as usual with house affairs, and was suddenly informed, about 10.30, by a note saying that David would be returning with H.E. and his party for luncheon here—eight in all—and that I was to prepare the table, seats and trimmings while Slater's own servants were bringing food and drinks, and everything else that would be required. Slater always conformed with the accepted rule of the Service that the Senior Officers when on tour always entertained their subordinates, and not the other way round. This was a delightful and unexpected treat for me, and our boys having made everything that had been asked for ready I hadn't long to wait before the party turned up in three cars, just before 12.15.

They had divided up before arrival in order that H.E. could go first to the Ashanti village and the Zongo, and personally speak to all the people about the Government's policy and agreed decision on recruiting; D. had to interpret for Mr. Slater, which was a welcome task for him. The other members of the party were Mrs. Fuller (Fuller did not come), Colonel Heywood, a very keen and well informed soldier, Mr. New-lands the Private Secretary at Government House, a delightful tall fair man, and Sharman the P.W.D. Chief whom we had met in Coomassie last August. I sat on H.E's left during luncheon, and found him an extremely nice, straightforward Englishman of perhaps forty-five years of age. As he had Mrs. Fuller on his right to look after, I was fortunate to have New-lands on my other side; the soldier opposite was perhaps a bit serious but I expect he was thinking more of Bole than of Ejura where there was no trouble going on. Before they left at about three o'clock, D. managed to have a quiet personal talk with H.E. who was anxious to find out all about him, and seemed quite ready to understand why he had asked for either leave to join up in the Army or at any rate to get more day to day hard work than the District afforded in wartime. Although nothing definite could be settled there and then, it was suggested that a transfer to Accra and work in the Secretariat might be arranged—if so, D. would be at once informed by Fuller at Coomassie. Most unusually, there was a bad though short thunderstorm while lunching, but all went well. I at first was feeling out of my depth as entirely unaccustomed to a party of this kind—two people being the usual guests here, and practically none at Wenchi!

The last four days of March have not produced any particular happening to write about, but today, April 1st, has been full of fun and games. A fellow Wellingtonian named Prevost who is Head of the Police at Accra was asked by D. to come up and spend a week end with us, and we had expected him up yesterday. Having imagined that he would turn up in the morning, we had waited till well after our usual lunch time for him and then, wondering why we'd heard nothing, had sat down to lunch by ourselves. But all was explained when he appeared half way through, for the car bringing him and Migeod had given a lot of trouble on the road, which necessitated repairs on the spot. Migeod had dropped him here with us, for he was to be *our* guest, and indeed our first one in the sense of staying with us and not chez Migeod or at the rest-house. He had brought a boy with him, and a bath, so was easily made comfortable at the Martello Tower which was done up recently for that purpose. We, all three, went down to the Police barracks after tea for him to do an inspection, and then looked in on Migeod who came back with us to dinner. Today Prevost and David went out early on the chance of a shot, but found that the wet night had made the ground pretty useless from a shooting point of view, so determined on a good walk only in the cool of the morning, returning happy and hungry to breakfast; roses on the table, and a large loaf of home made bread made it all look quite homelike. We were all three bidden to lunch with Migeod who sent his car for us before midday. On getting in we found the seat lacked its cushions and that Prevost's half of the board broke through, and produced a notice 'April Fool's Day' when he sat down on it! D. and Prevost had to visit the Court first and have a police palaver, while I walked on to Migeod's shanty for a pleasant talk and congratulations on the successful April fooling. We then had an enormous feed on Palm oil 'chop', beer, and banana fritters, and very soon felt 'kwoshi', the Hausa exclamation for 'I'll bust if I eat any more'. We just about managed to get back to the house, and give Prevost time for packing before Migeod arrived in the re-furnished car to pick him up and take him back to Coomassie. After tea, a little gardening and church at sunset to complete a successful week end all round.

The 2nd April found D. very much the worse for wear as the rich palm oil 'chop' had prohibited sleep from 2.30 a.m. onwards, in addition to which hyenas had howled and monkeys had spent the time in the nearest treetops giving short coughing barks; as a result he wisely decided to remain in the house all day, having just sent Moussa off to the Court to inform Nortye and to start making arrangements for an Easter week end camp in the bush which we had suggested to Migeod yesterday. My day was spent quietly in letter writing, superintending a big laundry morning, and a gardening afternoon with fortunately no visitors to disturb our peace. Two days later we were back in the old round of Court all morning and office work after luncheon for D., while I collected all the things needful for our Easter camp as, with a guest, we wanted to have more delicacies than usual. One passer-by looked in, a Staff Officer of Colonel Heywood's, named Blackburn. He had been ten months in France from early in 1915 and had fought at Aubers Ridge where Charlie was killed on May 9th; he had found that those particular ten days caused the most awful total of casulaties he had seen, for the Germans were expecting us and ready to let us have it. But he did notice before he left France that the German morale had weakened, and that week by week the difference perhaps only slight was commented on everywhere. He himself was going to Tamale for a conference with the N.T. Chief Commissioner as to the chances of the Bole troubles coming to an end quickly. The other news we had concerned ourselves alone, and was not unexpected. It came in a letter from Fuller to David, informing him that the transfer to, and appointment at, the Secretariat in Accra had been approved by the Governor, and that we could expect to go at the end of the month. Ejura would be closed for a short time as Philbrick was due to go home on leave and that meant at least two other transfers to fill the gaps.

All the more reason for getting a week end shooting camp, as once on the Coast there would not be any rest or holiday until at least August; early on April 5th, therefore, we went through the usual procedure which initiated an early start from H.Q. but one not so easy as usual because our regular Moshi carriers had been sent North with the soldiers. However, we decided to take only one hammock, and recruited some rather decrepit looking carriers from the Zongo, and got away by 8 o'clock. Stops had to be made at the Court and the police barracks, and then at the Ashanti town for a word with the Omanhin about prompt sending of the recruits to Coomassie, and a reply to the Nsuta Chief who had written a note on that same subject from his area South of Mampon. These official halts dealt with, we had anticipated a quick passage to Asuman by the Nkoranza road but, some women appearing with loads of yams, the new carriers wanted to stock themselves with food for the camp and rushed to buy, for which D. gave permission but supervised it himself by insisting that the transfer of yams and money was done quickly and quietly without the usual haggling, or the exercise of 'might is right' as often happens in regard to the price. At last we really got moving, and in due course covered the 12 or 13 miles which landed us at Asuman. David was still rather seedy, and had a bad headache so he took the hammock, and I proceeded on foot, dripping as if I was in a Turkish Bath, but in a curious way rather enjoying the complete freedom of plodding along however tired with ones senses all on the alert for anything new, a perfume from a tree, a burnt ash whiff from black forest-fired ground, or the temptation of a shady patch of palms. There were hundreds of butterflies above and around marshy patches in hollows, or unconsciously painting pictures with their beauty against the grey trunks of the ficus trees, tortoiseshell, saffron, white, purple, a tiny mauve one, and black and green beauties—an entomologist's happy hunting ground but *not* (decidedly not) much of a wild beast's natural preserve. The last two or three miles finally conquered, we were reinforced by the local hunter who is staying in the camp with us though the carriers and hammock boys, all but three of them will have to sleep at the village which is only 4 miles away.

The camp was a fine cleared space (but near very doubtful looking water) and canvas sheeted huts, as well as grass-thatched ones, had been erected for our bedrooms, dining room, bathroom, etc. as well as for the servants quarters and kitchen; all rather fragile as put up in less than three days but none the less welcome. I relaxed at once in a long chair with a large glass of water (brought from Ejura!), but soon found it almost intolerable owing to the thousands and thousands of insects, flies, ants, and every other biting creature that has wings. By this time David was touched with fever and was certain that this place was no earthly good for hunting. Having dosed him with quinine and aspirin, I ventured a bath of the rather unpleasant water—and after a small dinner of roast guineafowl and fresh pineapple retired to my mosquito net in hopes of a reasonable sleep. This came off in spite of bull-frogs croaking, crickets chirping, and a bright moon lighting up the trees and the camp most of the time, but we obviously had to move to something better. While ourselves breakfasting, we sent Moussa and two hunters with some hammock boys, and Ali the cook, to locate and pitch camp at a more open and better spot some three or four miles further on, a small track the hunters knew of. We remained behind with the rest of our companions in order to see that everything was taken down, packed, and started off while we were there to see, and then follow ourselves. After lunching, all now being clear, we started for the new camp both walking for it was cooler and rather fresher than yesterday. It took us about an hour and a half, but it was more open country, and an easy track, ending up ¼ mile or so from the rough path the troops had taken for Bole after we had seen them in Ejura. Moussa and his fatigue party had already cleared a large and excellent space (it was an old hunter's camp) near a slightly larger and sluggish stream called the Agimasu, where the happy jabbering of the men working on putting up grass huts and screens had actually guided us from the main track by their sounds. D. had bought a goat for the camp when we passed through Asuman which had been slaughtered in the old camp, making it available for the followers when their day's work was done; they are all so loyal and helpful that they deserve and appreciate an unasked-for gift like that. Next day, April 7th, David was up at 5.30 and out with the hunters and Moussa on what is his last chance of a good day's hunting for a long time; I having arisen about 7.30 and spent time looking for my toothbrush, which was found under a water can, and then washed and dressed in a sort of Garden of Eden dressingroom which, if one stood up above the enclosed circle of sheets and bits of curtain, made one look like Venus rising from the sea, I busied myself with the commissariat—this being a real bush camp.

There were several things to get our labour down to, the first being a temporary house on the other side of the little river if Migeod joined us (which we hoped he would do), a note to be sent to him by Chimsi, secondly more yams and bananas to be collected by Donkwai and Braima from Asuman, while the rest of the team either cleared and tidied the camp as a whole, or cut sticks to be used in the evening on fires to drive the insects and biting flies away. Meanwhile Bawi and I took the Union Jack down to the place 400 yards or so away where the main track passes our turn-off corner. There we put up a notice 'TO SWEAT FLY CAMP'; 'NO TRAMPS OR BARREL ORGANS ALLOWED'; 'BEWARE OF YE DOGGE', for Migeod's guidance if he managed to come. The morning had dawned bright and golden with a breeze that seemed to sprinkle gold dust over the newly rainwashed green trees, and especially behind the guest-house which Sunyalima and the others were building—their strong back muscles shining across the river when the sun touched them. D. arrived back at 11.30 very hot and weary after a long chase and attempted stalk after two hartebeeste; he had fired at and missed an oribi, and seen a rather rare red-flanked duiker as well as heaps of bush-cow tracks; but more rain is badly needed· for softening the ground and tempting the animals to feed in newly grassed patches. After a short rest to cool off, he indulged in a shave and a bath, in which he was no sooner hidden when the noise of people talking was heard on the main track; this made me rush down and see what it was (Moussa, Mama, and Ali all accompanying me) to find that troops had bivouacked a little further up the road and that a tall soldier was coming past our corner at that moment. I asked him if 'white man live', and on his saying yes I sent him back which, a few minutes later, resulted in the appearance of an elderly first 'Loot'—Mr. Bussell. He was promptly invited to lunch and as promptly accepted, coming back to our camp with me and telling me all about the Bole story. The threatened rising was all over before the troops got there, the rebel Chief 'Ya Boom' surrendering without any need of force on our side. It had been, as surmised, that the French recruiting had always been forced recruiting by a sort of old fashioned conscription, and our tribes were afraid that the rumours from Ashanti that this method was going to be employed in both Ashanti and the N.T. would lead to resistance throughout the tribal Chiefs in our area. As it was things ended peacably, Mr. Bussell being sent off back to Coomassie with 96 soldiers to refill the force at H.Q.

without delay; there were of course also a large number of carriers. Captain Baker is to follow with the rest of the troops recently sent up, except for 25 or so who are at Kintampo with swollen feet and other complaints, while Mr. Sherriff, the Bole D.C., is down with blackwater fever.

At 2 p.m. we went down to the road corner and stood by the flag while the whole contingent marched past in single file at 'eyes right', soldiers, carriers, and all. It was an extraordinary experience for me, a white woman in a bush camp in West Africa during a great world war seeing the march past of a column of troops on active service ready for action, and complete with transport of all kinds, tents, food, ammunition, etc., but all human carried; neither mechanical nor animal-drawn transport of any kind. There were Yaundis, Moshis, Dagartis, and Mendis in a long sinuous line winding between green grass and trees. The men looked pretty fagged out, but we were delighted to see three white colour segeants, including Mr. Jones whom we had met and entertained recently at Wenchi. Once past the saluting point, all marched at ease, carrying their rifles with the butts over their shoulders as they always do with the Dane guns. We returned to our camp, quite excited at seeing the troops in that unexpected way and spent a happy evening, as did the hammock boys who had somehow caught about thirty good-sized fish in the stream; D. found them after sunset sitting naked except for loin cloths round a blazing fire having a feast of stewed goat remains, cooked fish and fu-fu which they had managed to pound out properly in a hollow tree trunk! This was accompanied by continuous and high-pitched chatter until 8 p.m. when we all voted for sleep, and silence reigned.

Next day was Easter Sunday, and I woke to find D. gone on his last day's stalking, and the air full of all kinds of queer gurgling noises, birds of course, but except for the sweet plaintive low whistle of the green pigeon they were rough and rather hoarse tones, disturbing not soothing. The hunters and their master came in early, as the bit they had tried was no earthly good, only a single bush-buck espied and that too far for a shot or even a stalk. Soon after D's return a small mail came in from Ejura by the hand of the bailiff, in which there was a note from the clerk 'Your worship, some man kill man last night in Zongo, Sir, am I to keep body till you come, Sir, or bury him, your worship, etc., etc.' Before luncheon we had a little Easter Service by the stream, and then lunched in the little house we had prepared for Migeod since he was unable to come now, having had to arrange and supervise the transport to Coomassie of the troops which had passed us yesterday. The usual enormous Sunday ground nut meal made us rest rather quietly till tea time, and David then went out on a short after-noon's sport-finding walk as, if it had not been for Migeod's inability to come, we would have remained here over Easter Monday; alas! it produced no result. The only successful hunters that evening being myself (one green pigeon), and the Moshis (more fish). Early bed, for we strike camp tomorrow.

And tomorrow, April 9th, found us breakfasting before day-light and the camp dismantled around us so that we were off by 6 o'clock, not without fond glances at what was probably our last camp in Africa (certainly Accra wouldn't give us one) on this tour, and last goodbye to the happy bush life; but to think of 'lasts' is unpleasant and melancholy always. Counting the extra miles beyond Asuman we had some seventeen to cover before getting into our own house where, with all our kit and servants with us on the road, luncheon would not be possible on first arrival. That was solved by Migeod who sent a message to say that he expected us for that meal before he personally had to return to Coomassie. All our men, whether hammock carriers or loads, cantered along in sheer happiness most of the time, and we were assiduously helped by extra men from Asu-man, and other neighbouring villages. They will all get a substantial 'dash' in money from us in return for the willing help in the last five days. I eventually reached home at 2.30, and found everything in perfect order, with good old Nubila and the policeman in charge beaming on me. D. was fairly well tied up at Court with the murder case, so by the time he joined me, much later, he was all out. The following three days had nothing special to record until midday on the 12th, when a strange D.C. named Wilson arrived in a motor from Coomassie bearing a note from the C.C. that we were to pack up and come down at once for our shift to Accra, and that the bearer, Wilson, was to take over from us.

# CHAPTER X

# By Sea to Accra

April 13th, Friday. Although we had always expected con-
firmation of our transfer at the end of the month, this peremptory order to leave here today was impossible to arrange for it
entailed not only handing over the District but also a complete
turn-out of the house and the packing of all our property,
clothes, stores, beds, books, staff requirements, and ourselves!
We despatched a note to the C.C. saying we would endeavour
to move down on Monday, and while D. took Wilson to the
Court in the afternoon I began to organise the packing and
sorting of our many possessions.

Having arranged to quarter Wilson in the Martello Tower
and started the boys on filling up chop-boxes, luggage, and
packing cases, all of which we had retained from previous
moves, I accompanied D. and our new guest to the Zongo and
the Ashanti town after tea in order to explain the situation and
our imminent departure. On the way back we visited the
compound where the murder had been committed, and also
took a look at the two men who had been arrested on suspicion
and were now remanded at the police barracks. One of them
was a very criminal looking fellow, but it will be an awful hard
case to prove. Next day was one of numerous alarms and
excursions not only in solving the problems of our personal
packing and in D's case of handing over the office, but also by
reason of first the arrival of a young D.C. named Poole on his
way to the N.T. and later a belated entrance of Prevost who
had hurried up to investigate the murder case, but had broken
down several times on the road. We had young Poole to
luncheon, and were greatly amused by his bicycle which after

great difficulty he had managed to get painted white; this has resulted in his being offered three of four times its value by African after African wherever he stops by the road or in a village! He also supplied us with a good deal of home news and information and then departed to the rest-house, where in the evening he had Wilson to dine so that Prevost could join D. and myself in our own house. On Sunday Migeod came up for the day to arrange transport for us, invited us to be his guests at Coomassie, and then took Prevost with him in the afternoon. We managed to complete all our final packing, had a farewell walk round the garden, and eventually retired to bed rather early in order to be ready for the morning's last look at our Ejura home.

Monday, April 16th. We had expected to start about 1 p.m. —I having spent most of the morning dipping into the pages of a fascinating and famous book Wilson had with him called 'A description of the Gold Coast and Guinea' written by William Bosman in the latter half of the 17th century. He was a Dutchman, and the book a translation; it was adorned with cuts of birds and old forts on the Coast, and was most entertaining. But when instead of the private car all that arrived was the big lorry, our faces fell as it meant five hours in that cramped front seat unable to move and being jerked about continuously; our luck however was in for the lorry was soon followed by our P.W.D. friend Sharman who was driving Dr. Claridge en route to the N.T., and at once volunteered to take David and myself down (if ready) without delay. All was well, at least for the time being, and within an hour or so we were ensconced with Hankuri in the private car, and after waving goodbye to Nubila and Poiga who remain with Wilson we swept down the scarp and began to exchange the open country for the forest-belt. But our comfort and pleasure were short-lived for at mile 40 we came upon the big lorry completely broken down, the back tyres gone, and Ali, Mama, and two mechanics with masses of tools on the side of the road. A quick exchange of ideas was essential as everything we needed for the night was in cases on the lorry, and arrangements for the lorry load to be looked after for the night had also to be made, but in no time we salved the minimum we personally required to have with us. By good fortune we were then able to commandeer a

P.W.D. lorry to take everything else off the wreck and unload
at the Mampon overseer's house—while we went on, explained
the situation to the overseer, called on the Omanhin for David
to say goodbye to him, and dashed off down the Mampon scarp
into the cocoa farm country in the hopes of reaching Coomassie
before sunset.

Fate was once more against us; at mile 18 in a torrential
rainstorm the car stopped dead, went on $\frac{1}{2}$ mile at incredible
speed, and then gave up with no sign of life. A few moments
previously a native car had passed us, which Sharman as a
precaution had asked to stop whould we be unable ourselves
to proceed further. This was another bit of good luck for we
were undoubtedly marooned good and proper, but somehow
managed to get included in the passenger list of the native car
which on starting (with us on board) contained 3 solemn
Ashantis and 2 other men, David, Sharman and Hankuri and
my hat box, myself alongside the driver with Mama at my
feet on one side of me, and Sharman's driver at my feet on the
other! At least it was warm, and my big naval greatcoat made
my position fairly comfortable. When after dark we successfully
made Coomassie, the town with its bright lights looked on the
first glimpse of it like a vast curtain of fireflies, and we on the
front seat of a fire-engine. We dropped the three Ashantis,
drove round the Fort which was extraordinarily impressive
with its white walls and towers, and docked at Migeod's
hospitable house of the Reservation after a memorable journey.

We spent Tuesday, April 17th, in Coomassie, for although
Fuller had sent a message to us on arrival that it might be wise
to go straight on to the Coast today in case the steamer left
on the evening of the 18th, it was an impossibility after the
road troubles, none of our kit being with us and only reaching
us during the day. I welcomed this day off as on arrival last
August I had never really seen Coomassie or realised what a
large and interesting place it was, or how very well planned it
had been. D. having to call officially on the Chief Commissioner
and to visit the Bank and other offices also, I, escorted part of
the time by Migeod, did a tour (after a late breakfast) in a
fine hammock with four good Mendi-carriers. At the railway
station men were busy packing kola nuts in huge baskets for
shipment to Lagos, while the sheds were filled almost to the

roof with sacks of cocoa. In the afternoon David and I had an early cup of tea and then walked over to the Fort where we found Mrs. Fuller sitting at the tennis court. There were quite a few people there, Fuller himself, a Mrs. Wheatley (she had been in Sunyani during D's last tour), Dr. O'Dea, and M. and Madame Beaufils of the French Company; these two had been wrecked on the Liberian Coast on their way out, losing everything they had with them. We had a cool stroll back to the Reservation in the dark, with sweet perfumes from the flowers in various gardens; a quiet dinner and talk, particularly about poetry—Migeod is very un-West African!

The Coomassie mail train leaves daily at 6.30 a.m. and we were seen off by Migeod and Haltermann who shares the bungalow with him; also, but sadly, by Asetu and Bawi. Ali, Mama, Moussa, Tani and Fatima were coming with us to Accra, though Moussa then returns, being still on duty and as before will be at Ejura. The journey is dull and tiring with constant plunging into thick green forests and an occasional poinsettia's red flower in the undergrowth; there were various small stations, all with incredibly dressed Fanti women, one having her hair grown like a unicorn, straight out of her forehead. At a stop called Oponsu we happily got our home mail, for the Coomassie postmaster had asked the train postal van to sort out our letters on the way up from the Coast, and they were politely handed to us as arranged; the important stops were Obuasi and Taquah, at which the trains always stop a little longer for both have considerable industrial centres near, especially the Ashanti Gold Fields and other mines. Philbrick, former host at Coomassie last August got in at Obuasi as proceeding home on leave; but although we had tea with him in his carriage and a short talk, we carried on as we were for there were too many things we had to keep an eye on in our own compartment. We arrived punctually at Seccondee, i.e. 5.30 p.m., eleven hours for a journey of 169 miles—it is always said, not perhaps without a good deal of truth, that the line was built by contract and pursued the same sort of serpentine track that the ordinary bush path follows, doubtless when walking to avoid difficult ground and crossing rivers. At the station we were met by Mr. Williams the D.C., and the A.T.O. who was to check our heavy gear for Customs and shipment.

Empty bungalow No. 14 had been allocated to us for the night, a sort of normal lodging at Seccondee where, unless one has friends there, the passer-by is scarcely provided for since the only hotel is impossible. Our boys soon rigged up camp beds, and all we needed for the night—they themselves being quartered in the unused and empty dining room—while we were being entertained to dinner by Williams at his bungalow plus two doctors, one Dr. Ryan from the N.T., a droll Irishman, and the other a Dr. Macdonald from Axim. It appeared that the Elder Dempster cargo boat the 'Gambia' will be our ship tomorrow for Accra; all the more reason to retire early and be ready to go aboard as soon as possible.

After a very light tea and fruit breakfast, the A.T.O. sent a hammock and carriers for us at 8.30, it being Thursday April 19th, and with the boys and carriers we made for the Customs where, while D. was transacting the necessary business, I sat in a comfortable chair talking to the Collector, a very kindly man named Balston who afterwards accompanied us to the shore and sent us out in the Customs' own boat. The surf was not at all bad today; I seated myself in a basket chair on the sand and was carried out in it by four sturdy boys who heaved it with me, bodily, into the boat, while David holding on to the struggling Hankuri was carried out likewise. The boys uttering the usual peculiar sounds shoved off and paddled out a bit to where two other boats with out own boys and load were awaiting us, all three boats being then taken in tow by the ship's turtle-backed steam packet to the 'Gambia'. The mammychair was lowered, and we got in to be swung up on deck and dumped amid Kroo-boys, a surprised 2nd Officer, and a mixed cargo. The purser looked even more surprised, and said he was sorry but there was no accommodation for passengers. The one and only passenger cabin was occupied by a black parson bound for Winnebah. After a little deliberation he announced that as there was no Third Officer on board his cabin was empty and we could have that; meanwhile the Chief Officer offered me his neat little cabin to sit in, which I accepted with great pleasure and settled down on the plush sofa with the 'Daily Mail' and nearly fell asleep. On deck D. was busy seeing about our boys, Hankuri, our fowls, and the rest of the gear. We had lunch at 1 p.m. in the saloon, The Captain, First and

Second Officers, the Chief Engineer, the Purser, and the
Marconi Officer. 'Gambia' is a new ship, built since the war
began, about 4,500 tons; she looks very business-like, all grey
paint and wireless installations. The whole staff seem delightful,
and I was soon in converse with Captain Day, a sturdy hard-
working man of about 50, with sea-blue eyes and crisp curly
hair. He is typical of our sailors, has a cheery contempt for the
German submarines, one of which during his last voyage on a
foggy night he suddenly saw alongside him, equally ignorant.
Being about 420 feet long as against 'Gambia's' 350 feet, they
were easily visible to each other, but the German submerged
within seconds of his recognising her. Three of the crew had
been torpedoed off the Scillies a week before joining this ship,
and the 3rd Engineer, joining up while serving his apprentice-
ship, had been in France and through the Suvla Bay landing
before getting his discharge and going back to his proper work.

We sailed at 3 o'clock and steamed down the coast not far
out, getting a splendid view of Elmina and its old castle, while
8 miles further on we saw clearly Cape Coast Castle with its
magnificent big white fort situated on a rock washed eternally
by the waves. It at once made me picture the barracoons, the
sailing ships lying out awaiting the slaves they were to carry
to the Americas, and in the Forts of the camps the tippling
soldiery drinking their port and their brandy pawnee, and
dying like flies in peace or war, an existence which earned for
the West Coast the name of 'The White Man's Grave'. It was
terribly hot at night in the tiny cabin for there was almost no
breeze whatever, but in spite of that we both slept extremely
well, and on waking next morning found ourselves about a mile
from the beach at Saltpond. The surf there and at Half Assinec
is supposed to be the worst on the whole coast, but today was
fairly good with numbers of surf boats and lighters alongisde
for cargo discharge. The only excitment and problem was how
best to land two motor cars, and that done how to land a quantity
of cement! As to the motors, this was the method adopted.
Two large strong wooden planks were laid across two of the
surf boats and tightly roped; the crews then leapt naked over-
board, while the ship's derrick lowered the enormous wooden
cage that held one motor over the side and on to the plank;
the two crews then scrambled on to the surf boats again, undid

the hook which had held the rope round the box, let it go up, and then started for the shore with their paddles. Safely beached and unloaded they were soon back, and the amazing performance was repeated—one can't write 'smoothly' as, far from it, the surf boats were plunging up and down all the time and only the practised crews and the equally practised ship's company could have done it at all. As to the cement, I don't know the answer for at that moment the Captain insisted on bearing me off to have strong tots of lime juice and water—an age-old custom as an antidote to scurvy when at sea.

During the day we also touched at Winnebah where our African parson (the only passenger) was safely landed, and then just before sunset we reached Accra where the surf was absolutely terrible; nothing could come out to the anchorage, or go in, so with three other Elder Dempster ships we had to anchor and prepare to spend a rather uncomfortable night. When going to bed we were warned that this might go on for two days, or even more—'O rock and roll me over, only one more day', as the chantey has it. Our boys were rather divided in their opinion as to this queer voyage, Moussa, Tani and Fatima not enjoying it at all (even unable to eat, poor dears) but Ali and Mama quite fit I'm glad to say. Next day, April 21st, was obviously no better as, when waking, I could see from my bunk one moment the long line of Accra and its white buildings and, alternately, the roaring foam-decked sea which blotted out the porthole glass; this was followed with some difficulty by a bath, holding on to taps in bad heaves and at last managing to get to the saloon where I'm bound to say I did eat a hearty breakfast. All this time there was a noise of chipping and hammering as in a shipyard, but in this case meant mearely the activities of a crew in seizing any available chance of finishing off bits of the ship which had to be left over when commissioned in a hurry, as they all were in war time. The food was good, and one could even get really cold things since they had a refrigerator which the steward called the 'fridge', a word I'd never heard before.

There was no touch whatever with the shore all day, in spite of continuous signalling by the three other ships which were storm-bound as we were. During the day the 'Obuasi' which had lain inside of us moved out past us for she could not risk the chance of hitting the bottom in the rise and fall of 10 feet which is what we were having unceasingly—a ship in 30 feet of water might easily touch in a particularly severe plunge or roll. The pleasure of the day to me at any rate was the chance (and happening) of talks with real sailors who had been brought up in sailing ships, which was the case with the Captain and his First Officer. Captain Day himself had been on board the 'Golden Fleece' which came in second on the famous tea race in 1885, won by the 'Star of Greece'. There were forty-nine ships in it; both the first two did it in 75 days and only sighted each other once off Cape Agulhas before they entered the English Channel. The First Officer, who had gone to sea at the age of nine as a cabin boy, was aboard the sailing ship that collided with and sunk the French 'La Bourgoyne' in 1889, 800 lives being lost in Mid-Atlantic; he was an elderly very tough man with two medals of the South African war for which he had left the sea and enlisted in the Army, and then returned to a sailor's life—oddly enough he wishes it was still a sailing ship he was serving on! The Captain was full of anecdotes and experiences (11 months once in a South American port waiting for orders), and knowledgeable as to the chanteys and above all the old names for the sails used by the crews of the nineteenth century and earlier—'Jimmy Greens', studding sails, ring tails, water sails—there is music in the very sound of these names. Where are the fine ships today? 'The Golden Fleece' a bad weather sailer was lost, 'The Cutty Sark' a fine weather flier is now Norwegian with a crew of sixteen instead of forty-two; 'But the cargo that they carried was not only China tea, they carried all the glamour and the romance of the sea'. The other officers were much younger, but nice, quiet, and hardworking. As to our crew, it is a real mixture; two Russians, a Norwegian, a Rumanian, and a Dane, with a few British—and the rest African, Kroo-boys, Mendis, and Liberian.

Sunday, April 22nd, was no luckier, for the surf was still so hopeless that the 'Kaduna' which arrived in the morning had to go on to Lagos after a quick visit from the Customs boat. Reading and writing, chess and other games, with some serious study of Hausa in preparation for the exam D. has to take soon after our arrival, made the long hours pass quite speedily; at dinner and afterwards both the old sailing ship officers opened

up again on their experiences, one particular remembrance
being the period of 'piebald crews', one watch white and one
black, encouraging keen rivalry in the technique of setting sails
where every minute counts towards success. David was encouraged to talk about his years in Burmah and Siam working
in the teak forests, when he heard from Captain Day of the tea
clipper 'Sir Lancelot' (only lost a few years ago) built entirely
of teak, without a single flaw in the wood from bow to stern.

The sea moderated during the night, and we had hardly
finished breakfast on St. George's Day (April 23rd) when the
Customs boat was seen coming out towards us. We watched
her come, appearing and disappearing over the vales and
hollows and hills caused by the swell, and from the African
Skipper of the boat on arrival we were greeted warmly with
the words 'We have come for you'. Our boys and some of the
crew got quickly down to the collecting of luggage and other
impedimenta from the hold as well as the cabin, the fowls being
an important item, as also Hankuri. The First Officer was
sending a boat ashore to bring sand and other needs back which
made it possible for all our gear and staff to travel in her, while
David and I, with Moussa and Hankuri, could remain together
in the Customs boat without being cluttered up by luggage.
It was with very warm thanks of their unremitting hospitality
that we said farewell to Captain Day and the whole ship, after
which we were in turn lowered over the side in the mammy
chair to the diving boat below, always a bit of a thrill, as it
banged into the ship's side once or twice and had to make three
shots before settling us on the forepart of the boat. Once safely
on board we were rushed off shorewards, a distance of two miles
at least! It was magnificent riding as it were on a sea-horse's
back over the blue-green breast of the sea. Our boatmen,
five-a-side, were superb specimens of African manhood sweep-
ing the short paddles downwards and scooping the water in
perfect time; the coxswain, a fine looking man with a black
beard and gleaming white teeth, stood erect in the stern wielding a long oar as tiller. Nearer the breakwater the waves got
bigger, but oh! the final glorious lifting rush as we got into the
surf. Our coxswain stamped his feet smartly and yapped out
orders, the men responding with grunts and queer sounds and
a redoubled quick timing of their sweeps, the spray flew around

us like mist, there was a foaming, surging, living feeling about it all, and one felt like a disembodied spirit. It was just one of those moments when life seems at its zenith; I only knew that I wanted to shout for joy like the sons of the morning. All too quickly the few supreme moments were over, and we careered more leisurely round the breakwater on long rollers, gliding towards a flat sandy beach. The men cast all their paddles into the sea, jumped in themselves, hauled the boat up as far as it would go (one of them collecting the paddles), and I in my chair was lifted out and deposited on the beach smiling broadly on the gratified coxswain who apparently doesn't often get people to enjoy shooting the surf. We made a quick visit to the Customs, and then in the P.W.D. car sped past the old St. James Fort, still with its ancient bristling cannons showing over the ramparts, the new Secretariat, and several huge shops, to land at our new home in the European reservation at Accra.

# CHAPTER XI

# Secretariat Life Under Clifford

It is now May 1st, and we have been over a week in our new home, entirely ignorant of the new life one must lead here as compared with that which we have enjoyed for the last eight months. I would not have believed that, in a journey of less than a week and a mere two hundred odd miles as the crow flies, we could feel such complete strangers. But the few notes I have made since arrival, and the kindness of all the people we have already met, have begun to interpret the duties and pleasures that this new life has for us.

Our bungalow (No. 67) on the Reservation is a two-storey building, swept by breezes, and set amid bare grass and sand, surrounded on three sides by other bungalows but in front has an uninterrupted view down past Christiansborg Castle to the shore and the blue line of the sea; to me it is heaven once more to be within sight and sound of it. Most of the days have been occupied for my part by unpacking and arranging our possessions, helped of course by Moussa, Mama and Tani, while Ali who luckily knows Accra already is handling the marketing side; of David I have seen comparatively little for he rushes off to the Secretariat after an early (7.30) breakfast, and although appearing for luncheon between 12.30 and 1.0 he returns to the office till 5.0 or later. The persons he has most to do with, Mr. Harper (the Assistant Colonial Secretary), Mr. Farrer and Mr. Slater (the Colonial Secretary) have all been very helpful to both of us, not only in explaining his duties at the office but also in hospitality to us from the very start—it was indeed not until the third day that we had the first private meal in our house. It had not been occupied for some time, and a great many things had to be supplied by the P.W.D. before we could get going properly. Most of the principal Europeans seem to have cars for getting about, while some of the men use bicycles up and down to the office as David does.

There is also a go-cart, a kind of rather clumsy rickshaw, which one of our new friends has lent to us so that I can be taken down town to do shopping, or go to the Club, drawn by a strong Moshi named Naba who also puts in a bit of garden work. There has never been a proper garden, and we are already planting a few flowers and also some needed vegetables, at the same time wiring in a chicken run for the fowl we brought from Ashanti. Alec Norris, our predecessor at Ejura, is now in the Gold Coast Regiment and has already dropped in to see us with a Mr. Truell who works in one of the Secretariat departments, a most amusing Irishman from Co. Wicklow. On one of the days that I was busy at the house, D. and his Secretariat Chiefs with most of the principal Government Officers had to go down to the beach to meet Sir Hugh Clifford, the Governor, who was returning with his wife from home leave. From the house I could see the ship which brought them, resplendent with bunting under the brilliant sunshine, and it is perhaps a lucky coincidence for us to be the new arrivals on the Secretariat Staff just when H.E. arrives. It means working under new leadership by a fresh mind, relaxed by leave instead of perhaps an over-tired Chief longing to get away from it all.

Our Wedding Anniversary of 27th found us already being called on by several of the local residents, and we in turn calling on them—a thing that I had quite forgotten about but which is of considerable importance in Government circles here; fortunately we were able to have a nice little private celebration of our own, and spent the evening going over all that had happened since the 1916 arrival at Loch Goil with the salt water lapping the shore of the garden there until the present 1917 arrival on the ceaseless surf-ridden coast of the African Continent.

Alas! next day all Accra was saddened by the news of the sinking of the 'Abosso' somewhere off the South coast of Ireland; she had left here homeward bound with many Gold Coast residents at the beginning of the month, twenty or more from here, including two couples from bungalows near our own, and a much larger number from Nigeria. One couple from here are reported saved so far. It has been a bad week for us at sea, as the Germans claim to have sunk 40 ships in the last ten days; no wonder leave restrictions are imposed when possible.

The dining room of this house, or rather this type of bungalow, is like a station waiting room with drab distempered walls, green painted and glass doors, four plain wooden chairs, and a square table in the middle—one expects to see red-bound time-tables, Christian Heralds, and Railwaymen's Journals; it doesn't matter very much what happens to it, so we are not dismayed or unhappy at the storm which blew one of the windows out last night, and completely drenched all the papers, clothes, anything in fact that lay on the verandah that side of the house—we are told that these sort of storms are frequent here, so are now well warned and can take precautions in future. Lamps cannot be kept alight during them, nor candles even when protected, but at least we can and do appreciate the cool that is partially maintained on even the hottest of days. A similar storm blew up this morning, May 4th, which had been fixed for the Memorial Service at Holy Trinity Church for those who lost their lives in the sinking of the 'Abosso', and although for a short time the rain deluged the roads in every direction it fortunately eased down in time to permit the ceremony to be carried through. H.E. Sir Hugh Clifford and his wife, the Colonial Secretary, and all the European residents in Accra were seated in the front portion of the Church, and the African members of the Government Departments and principal business men in the seats nearer the entrance. All Government officials were in uniform, judges in their robes, and a guard of honour with a band of the W.A.F.F's. in full kit not only emphasised the importance of the occasion but also were responsible for the Last Post blown by three buglers after the Dead March and the National Anthem. The thunder from heaven oddly enough co-operated almost exactly with this final part of the service.

These terrific storms are very frequent at this time of year, but in between the ground dries fast, and whole days of sunshine give time for collecting plants for the garden, cannas in particular as they grow quickly and have a wonderful selection of colours. The quick growth applies also to Indian corn, sweet peppers, and other plants we must have for kitchen purposes; this work, or rather supervision, helps to occupy my time while D. is steadily becoming acquainted with his job at the Secretariat. It is all very different from the daily opportunities in Wenchi where we both could take a share of the problems in 'bush' administration. David has been having some more fever, partly due to his anxiety and swotting up Hausa for the Higher Standard exam which he had to take today (May 9th)—but all ended well as he came back to tea this evening having passed with 331 marks out of 400, 82.75%, a really fine result; the daily talks in the Ejura district, and the hours of practice with a teacher as well, have been rewarded in full.

Last Sunday we had managed to get a walk round the base of Christiansborg Castle, and saw the African canoes lying up in a lagoon under the eastern ramparts which in front stand sheer above a large rock and below them have the barracoons where the slaves were herded together before the sailing ships for America appeared to fetch them. It is a place full of history for at least six centuries, and one can well understand why the Dutch, the Portugese, the French, and ourselves all strove to gain its control. Miss Soward, a very nice girl who works in the Colonial Secretary's personal office, and Truell came with us—and afterwards all of us went to the 4.45 p.m. service in the Church where we had attended the 'Abosso' Memorial Service recently. The African attendance was remarkably good, and the clothes worn might have astonished Solomon, evincing every colour and shape that sould be invented! Being a hot afternoon, all the doors were open, through one of which the sea was clearly seen with the distant ships rolling at anchor, while on the land side there were some rather rugged sheep browsing on the long tufts of grass, not unlike the sights outside a Kirk in the Highlands! There was a good (though too loud) dusky choir, some with elegant shoes, others if boys with bare feet, but all in black serge surtouts, and very reverent. The old English rector preached a good sermon and then, for the final vesper hymn which was sung kneeling in prayer for our soldiers and sailors, the choir produced a really tender tone of voice and rhythm that was most impressive. We drove back under an avenue of gold mohur trees in the most glorious full bloom at the end of which the setting sun glided the breaking Atlantic rollers.

We were invited today by the Longhursts to go with them to Aburi and see the Government gardens there, Harper was going also, and we gladly joined them for the 23½ mile drive. Being a Saturday (May 12th) our Secretariat friends can get away at or after lunch time, and as Slater the Colonial Secretary was resting at the Sanatorium there the trip was most appropriate. There had been two bad rainstorms during the morning and our journey was a wild one for, although uphill nearly all the way, the roads were so wet that at times we roared through them as if we were in a motorboat race, clouds of spray on each side. Few houses to be seen and when seen they were rather tumbledown earth shelters—one of them gave us a hearty laugh for it had a notice board:—'Anna Maria Atishoo, Sweet-love Cottage', in large clear letters. It was so misty, and the road so hedged in by trees, that there was little to show that we were in Africa except for an occasional palm tree or a dusky figure standing by a hut. At last we turned off the main road into a fine drive of young royal palms and were soon disembarking at the house of Mr. Tudhope the Director of Agriculture who is in charge of this sort of miniature Kew Gardens. He comes from Peeblesshire and knows Glen which put us on good terms at once. Luckily the rain moderated so that we were able to walk about and be shown the various trees, plants, vegetables and experimental plots of which he was justly proud. Some of the plantations of limes, breadfruit, oranges, Botanga cherries, kola, and rubber were in splendid condition as were the fully grown royal palms and the Casuarinas which whisper in the breeze rather like pines or larch at home. We all left loaded with bananas, pineapples, grapefruit and avocado pears as well as lettuces; these indeed made it a very full car going home. The Longhursts and Harper were all dining at Christiansborg with H.E. so there were no stops on the way till they dropped us—but after a puncture half way they would only just be back in time to dress.

A week later, on May 9th, we had our first meal at the Castle, which was quite an occasion for H.E. always gives a series of such dinners on first arrival. During the previous four or five days I had a short recurrence of fever, but it cleared up quickly and enabled me to have two afternoons of tennis while D. was practising cricket at the nets; there is a small league of departments—Secretariat, Treasury, Legal, P.W.D., etc. of which Harper and David are the leading lights and a series of matches is being arranged in the next few weeks. Today there was another pretty bad storm, which made all the guests at Christiansborg slightly dishevelled by the time we arrived in the private rooms as there are three small courtyards on the way up between the ground entrance and our destination, but somehow with various squeals and agonised clutching of dresses (and heads!) we all managed to arrive a very few minutes after the appointed hour, and very glad to get there at all. Even after our welcome in the lovely big drawingroom with its lamps and sofas and photographs as at home, we had to make a dash across and along a verandah swept with rain (lightning flashing at the same time) into the temporary dining room, since in addition to the storm alterations are being made and have slightly isolated the main dining room from a service point of view. I was taken in by Judge Porter and found myself seated on Sir Hugh's left, he having Mrs. King Farlow on his right. From the very start the evening was genial and free from any officialdom; it felt just like home, greatly due I expect to Lady Clifford (Mrs. de la Pasture in the literary world) who is quite delightful in every way. From my seat I could see through the door to the open sea, lit up by the lightning with a small cannon standing out clearly against it. What a place to do Hamlet, and how well it would fit in with the historical memories in every degree; Lady C. has asked us to play tennis on the first fine day so we shall see it all properly then.

When the men joined us after dinner, we were divided into two parties, Lady C., Mr. Gosling, and the two King Farlows playing Bridge—while the rest of us under H.E's. control settled down to Poker at very modest stakes, having beans representing 3d. each to the total of 10s. each—for me the first time I had ever played it. H.E. and Newlands were partners, David and I, Mr. Maxwell and Bishop, and the Judge and Mr. Mackay—a rather sensible solution as more fun and more impersonal as to results. The Bishop is his crimson surtout and little cap had a greaty bushy beard and was smoking a huge cigar; he and Maxwell were at first pulling in the shekels continuously, and we all got a lot of fun out of it when Sir

Hugh once showed his hand thinking they (the Laird) as he is called out here and the Bishop) were no longer in, but then picked it up and said 'Go on'. At once Maxwell said, 'But I've seen your cards', to which Sir H. replied, 'Never mind, bet away'. 'Oh then' said Maxwell very quickly and earnestly, 'I'll bet the limit', whereupon David and the other men nearly fell off their chairs with roars of laughter for M. is well known as having a good name for 'economy' to put it kindly! In the end we managed to win 5s. on the evening; Sir Hugh called us 'The Young Boyles', and I loved him for that. When we left, the rain was falling gently but the darkness was stygian, there were few lights but we managed the slippery stone flights of steps and shining courtyards without mishap, and were driven home to stop at our corner when D. carried me to the door after a most enjoyable evening.

I had my first ride today on 'Punch', a steady old thing that Mr. Barton had lent me. Miss Soward rides several times a week if it is fine on her hours off, so today I was able to join her for a little tour round the cantonments, and the golf course; it was great fun, and even the bushes at the moment gave us a welcome with a sweet breath of frangipani from a great clump in the officers' garden. The following day I had an unusual pleasure in getting some practice on a baby grand, the first time I've seen a piano since last August at Coomassie; it belongs to a young wife who only arrived this year. The next good thing was the appearance of two workmen from the Director at Aburi with orders given them to re-design and re-plant our garden, and along the new drive that has been made. This was followed by three good sets of tennis at the Club, where though there was a rainburst in the early morning the courts played exceptionally well. It was Mrs. King Farlow's birthday, and we were bidden to dine there with them. Just before we started to go another frightful storm came on, but with Naba splashing along with me in the go-cart, Mama holding a large broken carriage umbrella over me, and David in sea boots by my side we managed to arrive at the house, where D. carried me in to dry in the verandah before being announced! Our hostess received us there, the Judge her husband being upstairs at the time, and then Dr. Le Fanu, Dr. Watson and Mr. Harper joined us, and we sat down to a first class birthday dinner.

After dinner Dr. Le Fantu, the Judge, and I sat together in a secluded corner and told each other ghost stories, the Doctor being rich in them as for three whole years he had lived in the hospital at Cape Coast Castle, and for some time also at Elmina. Both of these places are renowned all along the coast for being full of ghosts regularly seen to this day. He himself constantly heard noises, people walking about and breathing in his room, while one night he woke up to see a figure at the foot of his bed, then the mosquito net was tugged and afterwards he got two blows on the side of his head. The locals themselves often saw people walking on the sands, and children, (but when approached these always vanished completely) who were regarded as the ghosts of the drowned throughout the years. The rain was still pouring down steadily when we left about midnight and the night was as dark as ever, but we saw no ghosts and arrived home safely.

The following Saturday dawned wet and foreboding, but we were not too surprised at lunch time when a message came from Christiansborg that, tennis being impossible, would we both come up and dine, a quiet dinner with Captain Armitage who had arrived from home and wanted to see us again. This was glorious news and when Newlands the Private Secretary came for us at 7.20 we were as happy as schoolchildren going out on the spree and enjoyed every moment of it. The rain had stopped and there was a small moon and starlight which made the Castle more like Elsinore than ever. There were just six of us at dinner, the Cliffords, Captain Armitage, Newlands, and ourselves—H.E. having just received all the latest news from the wireless station was able to give us four sheets of Reuters, largely encouraging on all fronts except as usual in submarine areas where the 'Transylvania' had been sunk with 400 men; she was an Anchor Line used as a transport. Captain Armitage was in great form; he is always interesting both to the Cliffords and to us, for no one else now serving has such a complete knowledge of Ashanti and its people. He was there before and during the 1900 war and did the most dangerous and special jobs in it, and then was Chief Commissioner, but now acts as a sort of elder statesman to the Colonial Office on Gold Coast Colony's affairs as a whole. After dinner Lady C. and I had a quiet heart-to-heart for a while, and then the Cliffords,

Armitage, and David sat down to Bridge. Newlands and I were soon deeply engrossed with the war and political affairs to the accompaniment of the roaring surf beating against the rocks only 30 feet below! About 11.0 Newlands drove us home on what was normally a very quiet road but appeared tonight to be chock full of large toads who croaked and croaked, jumping in front of the car's lights as if it was an animal's pantomime.

One Sunday soon after that little Christianborg party I was taken down to the Secretariat to see the building from the inside, a convenient time as officially it was closed but there were always some senior officials there trying to cope with arrears. Harper and Farrer were both in their rooms, as were David and Miss Soward. It is a really good and handsome building, the Council Chamber being fine, cool, lofty and airy with some beautiful polished tables of the local mahogany and a covered verandah all round, with wide stone steps leading up to it from the courtyard below. In the afternoon we attended the Church again, glad of the sort of specially quiet home Sunday for once; in the evening this was made even better by a long talk with Farrer and Dr. Le Fanu on poetry and literature of all kinds.

The night was, as only too often, a wet one but sound as I slept I found myself at about 5.30 a.m. out of bed (and outside the mosquito net) on the verandah outside our room. The eastern sky was afire, the grass below just beginning to assume a greenish look but colours were indeterminate, and the ground darkened towards the horizon where it was still that velvety black; a few big trees like elms at home silhouetted against the golden-red sky which lightened and lightened as one's eye travelled from the horizon upwards. It seemed to be made of all the pale translucent colours imaginable, filmy blue, pale green, and primrose yellow. The undersides of the flocks of cloudlets were blushing with pink at the approach of Helios, and the bright morning star still shone clearly above the dawn but with increasing faintness. Out of the front window the sea was hidden by a veil of oyster-grey cloud and mother of pearl, part of it in shapeless cumulus clouds low down like a fleet of galleons in full sail. The surf broke with crescendo rolling as of a drum, into a long-drawn diminuendo with the swell pedal down; the earth was empty, the world seemed on tiptoe as if the presence of a human being would break the exquisite spell. I climbed back into bed, and from there saw the sun burst his prison bars to rise like a conquering phoenix into the morning sky. So I slept again, having seen the vision glorious.

This May and June period seems to be rather like the London season so far as Accra is concerned, and while still keeping a pretty careful diary will just have to compress into less detail the happenings that ensue. May 31st for example appears to be the start of the cricket season, and most of us including H.E. and Lady C. watched the first day when the Secretariat played the Treasury with two of our own Civil Service on each side. David (Capt.) and Harper were the Secretariat two, and they won the toss. D. came out with a duck first ball, Harper 8, and two of the African clerks 45 and 56—but the total was only 138, the Treasury having one really good fast bowler and the fielding being excellent. As well as cricket, there are Lawn Tennis tournaments, a Bridge tournament, Golf, and a tiny Polo session—all of which keep people busy when not in the offices. They don't play the long hours we have at home, for it is too hot on many days and too wet on others. For more sedentary occupations there is an excellent Red Cross Committee presided over by Lady Clifford, another Committee for Children's care, and a number of musical, sketching, and literary groups. The Chief Justice, Sir Philip Smyly, a Dublin family, has just arrived from leave and is a keen lover of books and gardens, very good company in every way, and has already called on us. As to the Army, there are constant changes at the W.A.F.F. barracks where Colonel Potter holds the reins skilfully, not an easy job with a war on; the question of reinforcements for the battalion in East Africa plus training recruits here leaves little time for recreational or social life in a trophical country rife with malaria and other illnesses. I have just made the acquaintance of the main Hospital Staff, where there is a most capable and charming Matron and three good Sisters; the doctors belonging to it are the ones I've already met and are a fine lot.

June 3rd. One of my new friends, Mrs. Harrison, has a very accomplished husband who paints and sketches exceedingly well. He had promised to do me one of Christiansborg Castle, a splendid present to have and keep as a reminder of my life here; it will be done in sepia. After a pleasant and artistic luncheon with the Harrisons (she can make both a table and what is on it to eat things of beauty) I went to visit my riding companion, Miss Soward and found her in bed with malaria, then back home to find D. down similarly and Dr. Le Fanu having already told him he can't play in the second half of the cricket match which is due tomorrow (the King's birthday and therefore a holiday). It is now June 9th and I am bound to say that there has been a sudden outbreak of malaria all round; during the last five or six days D., although up twice, has been quite bad at times and I had one bad day myself. In his case we had to bring his Bridge tournament companions up to play with him in bed, which turned out all right for him, he and Bowerley winning their match easily. As the Secretariat won the unfinished cricket match on June 6th he was feeling quite cheered up and has begun to cope with office boxes brought up from the Secretariat by messengers. The kind Harrisons took me a walk this afternoon to see the old Slave House in the village near here and learn more of its history before the slave trade ceased. They are the sort of poeple who soon look into (and get to know) the real facts and history about their surroundings, unlike the ordinary temporary official who hardly ever takes the trouble to find out such things. We turned off the road near the shore into the dilapidated and rather unpleasantly dirty village called Christiansborg. The houses, or the remains of them, had obviously been quite reasonably good, but as Accra began to prosper the former inhabitants probably drifted steadily into the new town. In spite of the dirt, the large but empty market, and one or two unkempt streets, there were many parties of African clerks and others walking with their girls whose hair is frequently worked into wonderful chignons covered with gorgeous handkerchiefs—around them wander goats and kids, mangy pi-dogs, and naked children. We passed a quaint little white square house in the middle of an open space which possessed a door and no windows like a closed-in well. Mr. Harrison called it 'The Treasure House', and said that the Christiansborg Chiefs in the old days kept their money there, but a village elder when asked told us it was a gunpowder storehouse and is now used as a Fetish house. As these people never give anything away in that field, we did not ask any more questions. From there we went up a fine red road bordered by trees and coconut palms, and by slow degrees reached the old Slave House. A stone gateway of the conventional Queen Anne style led into an open courtyard, where there was a carved stone over the doorway with the initials C.R. and I.R.—1809. This opened on to a stone verandah with rooms behind it. Around the courtyard there were curved arches giving on to vault-like places with narrow apertures which were the only means of daylight, but the roofs and ceilings are now all gone and everything is open to the light of day and fast rotting. This was Richter's house and its secrets are buried with it—even the several African families who lived in a sort of fringe encampment around it know, or tell, nothing of its history. There were Germans in those days at the Basel Mission, and we saw a child with definitely European, perhaps German, features; the 'Slave House' name was probably given to it before the Richter concerned lived there. From a little hill above all this we caught a perfect view of the Castle perched on its rock with the surf breaking around it, an incredibly beautiful clump of tall palm trees just on the left. It was close on sunset and we walked slowly back past Richter's house, now bathed in mysterious gloom, and didn't talk much till we reached the main road and could see our respective homes.

June 13th. Leaving D. still in bed after breakfast I did a brisk walk to leave a note on Mr. Crowther at his house, stopping on the way to watch the lovely little cardinals, very bright red birds, hovering over our lawn and perching gracefully on a swaying stem to plume themselves. They have sheeny black heads and waistcoats, fiery red necks, back, throats and ruffles—they look just like rubies with the sun on them. On my return I found the Doctor there, who said the patient could get up for luncheon—the first meal up for some days, so that was encouraging. After going up to the hospital for tea with one of the Sisters there, I did a good walk down to the Club where the band of the W.A.F.F. which had been doing a recruiting tour was giving a farewell of music before returning to Coomassie. The Cliffords, Harper, Crowther and I all sat together, and for a few moments felt quite back at home with 'Puppchin', the 'Valse Triste' and other melodies. Roger Hall who had been at New College with David, and is a barrister out here, joined me later—a new arrival with a refreshingly new mind on politics and books. I found D. a lot better so it was a good day all round.

The 'Appam' the ship which D. luckily had missed when coming on leave in February 1916 arrived back yesterday, June 14th, morning from America via Sierra Leone with 800 tons of stores for the West Coast. After leaving here (without D. who had a go of fever) in 1916 she had been captured by the 'Moëwe', all the males of military age being put on board a submarine to be taken to Germany, and the ship herself taken to the U.S.A. for internment. Now that America has come in she could be legally released by them and, luckily escaping her old captor who is again in the Atlantic, has bravely reappeared in the ports she knew so well. Lying alongside her is a four-masted American schooner, one of a number which have been trading here and taking back rum and other products including mahogany to the U.S.A. since the war began.

June 17th. There has been a small rising of the Ningos, a tribe living some 30 odd miles East of Accra on the Coast; as a precaution 100 police with two guns were despatched yesterday to Prampram, the chief town of that area. There was once a castle at Ningo itself build by the Danes in 1734, but that is now in ruins as is the one at Prampram built by us in 1802. The importance of these forts in those days was that the Coast as a trading area spread from the mouth of the 'Tano' on the West to Adda just short of the 'Volta' river on the East; but after the early years of the nineteenth century they were of no value. This piece of local history was gleaned by me out of Dr. Claridge's 'History of the Gold Coast' to which I alluded once when at Wenchi; it is a veritable storehouse of 600 years' information.

# CHAPTER XII

# War News Accelerates Departure

June 19th, when this last extract of my diaries begins, finds us fairly well settled down at Accra, for we have made a great many new friends here. It is rather a dull and even unnaturally comfortable life compared with the changing days of our Ashanti months, but the fact of living by the sea and being very soon due for leave makes the days pass quickly. This afternoon Lady Clifford presided over an important Red Cross meeting up at Christiansborg to which Mrs. Harrison and I with six or seven others I knew had been invited. It was to decide the programme for a Red Cross meeting this October, and every suggestion or idea was welcomed and closely discussed. Mr. Slater took us up in his car for as Colonial Secretary he had to be consulted in many ways. D. was not on the Committee, and anyhow was umpiring in the Lawn Tennis Tournament for the match (doubles) in which Sir Hugh was playing. This is David's second full day up after his nasty week of fever, though he still is not permitted to take exercise himself which is bad luck as it prevents him playing cricket in the best bit of the season.

Both mail steamers out and home were in port today, our own mail being quite unusually large, in fact I had 21 letters myself! It is amazing how inured we are now to the complete absence of daily posts or newspapers, but at least on the Coast there is Reuters to fill the bill as to war news. I had another good ride this afternoon with Miss Soward who had been secretary at the Red Cross meeting this morning; we fairly flew round the racecourse, hats blown off and a real attack of speed by 'Punch' who is generally rather sedate. After changing and

tea at home I remembered I'd not seen Tani this morning, so
went over to the boys' houses and found that the poor little
girl had developed guinea worm in both her legs and couldn't
walk at all. I was so sorry for her lying on the floor on a mat
under a small mosquito net; after we had a little talk about it
in Hausa, I promised her that Doctor Le Fanu would be asked
about it as soon as he could be got hold of. D. had been visiting
his partner (Bowerley) in the Bridge Tournament, who like so
many others just now is laid up with a go of fever.

The visit to Bowerley the other day seems to have been
successful, as the latter was up and about again today, June
22nd, and with David succeeded in winning their match against
H.E. and Lady C. in the semi-final of the Bridge Tournament
after a tough fight. Before going up to the Castle to play, D.
had a most interesting and enlightening talk with Harper who
being Assistant Colonial Secretary can inform and advise his
juniors as to promotion, leave, and transfers on a private level;
he is so charming, so efficient, and so popular that even if his
advice is unwelcome, it can never be resented or discounted
by the one who asked for it. The position seems to be that The
Colonial Office has decided that there should be no promotion
until the end of the war, and that numbers of the Services in
all Colonies will be retiring or resigning at that time. But while
that means many vacancies, it also means (at any rate in this
Colony) that although David is now 3rd or 4th from the top of
his grade, there are a dozen below him who will be promoted
at the same time as he is. Obviously not fair.

Neither time, distance, nor place can upset the inherent
instinct among country lovers of going round the garden on
Sunday morning, and it was natural today that we both seized
a hat after breakfast, (I taking one of David's topees!), to cruise
round our patch, (*not* cabbage here), admiring our newly
planted shrubs, box edgings, and flowers with a special eye for
the pathetic little farm Ali has made behind his house in order
to produce home grown vegetables. This is already of considerable value for there are corn plants, small onions, ground nuts
and 'dankali' sweet potatoes, a toothsome root which I much
relish. There are quite a number of edible fungi to be got also,
but we were lucky to see some as our old garden boy, a recent
acquisition, does not come on Sundays, and there never seem

to be any on the days he has been! Longhurst called for D. a little later and the two of them went down to the Secretariat to cope with some outstanding files urgently requiring action. In the afternoon we went to church with the Longhursts, it being the last Sunday that the old Rector will be there before he retires for good. With Miss Soward, Truell, and two dogs I then started off for the Christiansborg sands, and after a scramble there on the overhanging rocks we paid a visit to the old cemetery beside the Castle walls where 7 or 8 Danes and one Englishman had been buried and have headstones; other and older graves have all got smothered by grass and weather. There was one grave in a far corner by itself—N. Lessingham Bailey, 1886—it did not describe who he was, but two Danish governors both young in the thirties, Ludwig Vincent von Hein, 1831 and Bernardt I. C. Wilkens, 1842, were in another part, and there were also two headstones to Danish women. It was very sad to us three young ones of the present day to meditate among the tombs of those who seem rarely to have passed into their forties; but sanitation and proper medicines were unknown in their days.

We woke up very happy on this Wednesday, June 26th for D. had with his partner Bowerley won the final contest in the Bridge Tournament last night after a really long struggle. This happy feeling was intensified at lunch time for he returned from the office where Mr. Slater had officially told him that we could proceed on leave after we had done our 12 month tour which means August 3rd; there was doubt about it, and also about the Harrisons, because Admiralty restrictions still apply to women travelling during the submarine menace; Slater however refuses to listen to that for his answer is 'There is no provision made out here for temporary "widows"'—so that was that!—and even more luck, as we were sitting down to luncheon a couple of Hausas arrived selling cloths, mats, and animal skin among which David spied a Kitta cloth, the one thing I have always longed to obtain and particularly now when we are so near the town where they are made. We both leaned over the verandah looking down at their goods spread out on the ground below and after a talk in Hausa with one of the men it was arranged to send up anything we thought of buying by the hand of Mama, who promptly joined the game.

The cloth in question was a lovely one, very large and made up of squares of dark blue, orange, yellow, white and red with a fundamental blue through which ran a thin white stripe from end to end. The salesman below then lavishly described the cloth's beauty, its rarity, and its price; to this D. contemptuously cried 'Alberka' equivalent to 'not having any!' Again the desired price, £3 10s. was submitted by the vendors, both pouring out their opinions of its unparalleled beauty and durability. This ended by a final 'no—can't buy at that price', the cloth was cast over the verandah, all the goods packed up, and the merchants disappeared down the drive. Hardly had they gone, when a hasty conference took place with Ali and Mama which resulted in Mama being sent after the men and told to offer £2 10s. Back they came, and after a bit more amusing chaffering the men requiring £2 15s., it was sold to us for £2 11s. When writing a cheque for £2 15s. D. said they could pray to Allah on the way to the Bank, and perhaps find that after all he had honoured them with an extra 4s.

We have now really got something to take home which is worth having and can adorn our house for many years; the same cloths can be, and are occasionally, made in silk but then are priced at £15-£20. Our friend the Omanhin of Tekiman had one which naturally is of lighter weight and only worn on special occasions. The last few days I have had several small bouts of fever, and am particularly sorry for that as it has meant my being unable to say goodbye to Lady Clifford who with H.E. and his personal staff has left by sea this morning, June 30th, for Seccondee where the new waterworks are to be officially opened, and followed by a short tour of the coast ports from Axim back to Accra. Newlands, Harper and Longhurst are of the party, but Slater meanwhile holds the reins as the Colonial Secretary automatically does in the Governor's absence. In the afternoon it was the 'officials v. unofficials' annual cricket match, Harper and David being absentees from our side; the game was very exciting and ended in a victory for our team by 9 runs just as darkness fell. We had Sir P. Smyly the Chief Justice, Mr. Kitson geographical Director, and the interesting Crowther, Secretary of Native Affairs, to luncheon today which meant most varied talk on subjects in no way akin to the normal local jargon, and made one feel more in the world and less in a small outpost.

July 4th had been mentioned very often recently as it was to be a total eclipse of the moon, but on waking up the sky was black or grey, the rain torrential with some thunder, and with one brief interval this funeral atmosphere lasted from 8 a.m. to 6 p.m.—The interval was just at lunchtime when there was a clear vista to the far horizon over the sea, and thinking it odd that a sort of smudge could be moving I snatched our field glasses from their peg to see with real wonder a French cruiser or warship of some kind! She had four funnels, two near the stern and two near the bow; we presumed she was on patrol from Dakar, but it intrigued us greatly as there had been no talk of French naval vessels out here at all in our time. The rain was so furious again after our meal that David couldn't get back to the office at all; luckily his schedule is the P.W.D. in which great economies are being insisted on during the war and therefore the work is lighter than usual. To watch the eclipse we had four guests to dinner, and at 8 o'clock when they arrived the full moon was quite visible but not in a really clear sky. By 9 o'clock it was a faint kind of copper with a smoky black shadow creeping over it and then for a time completely dark—after which a full clear yellow and normal again. I wish it could have been a really clear night for that would have made it more interesting and in this right setting over the sea, more beautiful.

It is now ten days since I last wrote any particular notes of things worth recording, partly because they were few and far between and partly owing to a sort of silence all round, news, entertainments, illness, and (in my case) little real interest in. anything but home leave and that as quickly as possible. It is now July 14th—the Governor and Lady C. have cut their tour short owing to bad weather and arrived back this evening, the home marine news is bad in regard to our mail service, the 'Taquah' sunk but no lives lost, the 'Akabo' hit but escaped, and an uncertainty in other cases. At H.E's request D. had during his absence visited Christiansborg two or three times to see all was well in the Garden and Tennis Court, and one of those days was just after the Eclipse. It is worth recording because we both were surprised to find there on duty two previous acquaintances, in one case the corporal on guard

(Seidu Wangara) had been the under-warden at the Wenchi prison, and in the other instance a young Ashanti recruit from Mampon where we had held that ticklish meeting on the recruiting campaign. Seidu was so pleased to see us and to have a talk in Hausa, while the Ashanti lad seemed to think it the last word in luck to be able to talk his own Twi language to someone who also knew his home town. We took the opportunity of visiting all the courtyards, and the main garden which was more of a pleasance than a flower garden and had one or two good shade trees affording a quiet corner well away from the busy house and windswept terraces. We missed Newlands who was away with H.E. for he would have been an ideal companion in and around what D. and I call our 'enchanted castle'; I wonder what his next appointment will be, for of all the young Civil Servants we have met out here, he stands head and shoulders above the others in character, brains and attraction. Both H.E. and Lady Clifford are a bit under the weather as a result of the recent tour, and Dr. Le Fanu has been called in to overhaul them. It amused us to learn that in the last stage of the tour they had to return from Cape Coast by the 'Accra', a sister ship of our 'Gambia', but as we know probably not all that comfortable. Harper of course as well as Newlands returned with them, so the Colonial Secretary's staff is more or less 100% on combined duty again.

While their Excellencies are remaining rather quiet in Christiansborg, I am doing the same thing though with rather more actual bouts of malaria and high temperatures at our own home; it is today July 20th, and I succumbed to the beastly thing less than forty-eight hours after writing the above paragraph. What is much more serious is the news today that Crowther is down with yellow fever, as is another younger man, and one woman; the facts were officially notified this afternoon and there will be great anxiety in many places. Mr. Crowther apparently got this awful disease at Ningo where in his capacity as Secretary of Native Affairs he had been investigating the causes of the small rising there which I mentioned at the end of chapter 11 as occurring or reported on June 17th. The other and younger sufferer was also from Ningo where he had been on the same case. The last news tonight is that Crowther is through the crisis; we do hope he will pull through for he could ill be spared in his job, he is a welcome and grand guest, and more important than all that is a married man who is due for leave next month, and has only had 5 months leave in the last 4 years. Two days later, July 22nd, we woke up slightly sleepless owing to a very noisy night in the Christiansborg village streets where the younger generation were celebrating the annual 'Yam custom' holiday, and had been doing so most of the day; even the most prim and well dressed clerks go traditionally mad in excitement on those occasions and they don't have to ask for a 'pass' after 9.0 p.m. as they had to do at Wenchi.

Being Sunday we had a little ground nut midday meal, D. having been out on a private visit to the Crown Counsel, a man named Macquarrie, from whom he wanted some help and some coaching on his coming Law exam which is known to be rather a tough hurdle. After luncheon we both lay up for a bit, and on arising from our Sunday siesta noticed that the flag on the Castle was at half-mast. On going across to the nearest neighbour for explanation, we learnt as we had feared that it was Crowther, who only a week ago had been at lunch with us and full of life and humour. Later in the day Greville, the younger man, also died but the female case, (we don't know her name), is apparently pulling through—an odd thing which appears almost to be a rule in 'Yellow Jack' cases. Both the men were buried early next morning with as little pomp and ceremony as possible. It is best so out here. It was a beautiful day, palms waving, red and white roofs shining in the sun, and the sea ruffled by a gentle breeze and the plucky little 'Akabo' outward bound with mails for us anchored near the American schooner with her Stars and Stripes at the jigger-head; her four tall tapering masts are most imposing on a day like this. After the funeral D. had been to the Secretariat as usual, and returned wildly happy with the news that bookings had been made for us to go home by the 'Akabo' from here on August 3rd; we both simmered with delight, but he had to return early after luncheon to do his law exam from which he emerged at the Club very miserable saying the exam had been appalling, and he was sure he had failed. At home in the evening we soon began to talk about packing up, arranging to auction things we didn't want to take with us, write letters home with the news, and

generally start goodbyes with our friends here. The 'Akabo'
herself seemed to bring the luck with her!

Next day the Longhursts, who had been away three weeks
and actually stayed in our Ejura bungalow, gave me news of
all our friends in Ashanti. Mrs. Fuller had been very ill with
dysentery, Mrs. Wheatley with malaria, and only Wilson who
succeeded us at Ejura appeared to have no complaints and
was enjoying his post. Oh! Gold Coast, Gold Coast, not yet
have you earned the right to the name of an health resort—
I don't suppose we have another Colony with so many difficulties
as regards health and staff. It is hard for me to take a line on
it as I want to push out my right hand and withhold my left.
I long to see the best type of man out here in every capacity
for the natives' sake but it is difficult to recommend it as a
career to the suitable young man when one has experience
living here oneself. It is as yet no country for a young wife who
desires a home and children; it might mean years of two
houses, intervals without the wife, and illness making the
African side ot it almost prohibitive both to health and to
expenses particularly when there are children. It is a privilege
to have been out here and realised how one can be personally
proud of our Empire, and of what it and its servants are trying
to do, but it makes one sad to feel that at least for the present
the country is not everybody's home. Musing on these questions
I walked down to meet D. at the Secretariat in the Afternoon,
and was greeted with news that after all he had passed his
Law exam, and with 70%!

The next four days had little interest to be noted, except that
D. also passed the second and oral part of the exam with 60%
so has no more tests to bother with and his record is full. He
has had some good tennis, an afternoon with Mrs. Harrison
as partner playing Bridge at Government House with the
Cliffords, while both of us have been entertained or entertaining
at every meal; people like Sir P. Smyly, Harper, Slater, Farrer,
Miss Soward, and Truell will be remembered by us for a long
time, and indeed one can honestly say that there is no one here
we will not miss while in sight of the West African coast. Dr.
Le Fanu deserves a sentence to himself, while Mr. Barton and
I had a glorious gallop on 'Punch' and 'Pearl' this afternoon;
it makes me understand the Arab's view of life, 'Paradise is to

be found on the back of a horse and in the heart of a woman'. Sir Philip came in to tea with us and then drove us to the French Company's house where we again met the charming young couple M. and Mme. Beaufils last seen in Coomassie after their experiences of being wrecked and losing all their possessions. We had a pleasant hour talking French there, and were eventually brought back by Sir P. whom D. accompanied to his house for a further talk; I think he misses his wife very much and is rather lonely here.

I realised this morning that it was July 31st, and that meant only two full days for final packing, goodbyes, and clearing the house so far as our possessions were concerned. The future of our excellent staff had been a difficult one to make a decision on, but they were able to ease our minds by themselves deciding *not* to return on board wages to their respective Districts in the N.T. as they have always done for David, the war position and the heavy rains at this time of year being unsuitable for long journeys like that. They have individually arranged (warmly recommended by us) that Ali is going to Mr. Slater as cook, and Mama to Colonel Potter out at Cantonments. As for Tani, Mama was quite firm in his desire that she was not and indeed did not want to work for any other Missis because they wouldn't 'play' like me! I feel that it is the nicest compliment ever paid to me, and I reciprocate it to the girl of whom I am really fond. Hankuri is to be looked after by Doctor Le Fanu; Moussa of course is still at Ejura and anyhow belongs to the Police Force in the Ashanti and N.T. area. We are sending him some old clothes, and also passing on some things to our good Wenchi clerk, Osman. We ourselves have been so happy with all these people that it is hard to part with them; from Osman downwards they all rose to the occasion whenever travelling was difficult, weather catastrophic, and my illness rather more than serious. At least half, if not more, of our happiness out here has been due to them.

August 3rd and we completed a year's tour by embarking this afternoon on the 'Akabo' homeward bound, not exactly without a vague foreboding of difficulties as the 'Karina', (the last mail leaving from here), was reported this morning as sunk two days ago. Yesterday we paid a farewell call at Christiansborg taken there by Newlands who is acting as a housekeeper

and chief nurse to the Cliffords, both of whom being still laid up;
after which we drove out to Cantonments where Colonel Potter
and the other officers some seven in all gave us a scrumptious
farewell dinner party with a turkey the special feature, said to
be specially bred and fattened for the occasion! Back to our
dismantled house to sleep, and then today breakfast with the
kind Harragins, *and* luncheon also for the ship was rather late
in arrival. At 2.0 p.m. Mr. Harragin drove us down to the
beach where the surf was not so bad as usual. There the Customs
boat was awaiting us, and to the splendid rhythm of the sweep-
ing paddles, the songs of the crew, and the stern shouted cries
of the coxswain we were rushed out to the steamer's side, hoisted
up in the mammy chair and then stepped out of it on to
'Akabo's' deck about 3 o'clock—a very appropriate West
African departure, to me increased in memories by the 4-masted
schooner being anchored just beyond our bows. Our skipper,
whose name is Toft, was one of the 'Abosso' officers when she
was sunk in April. Mama, who had accompanied our baggage
to the ship said a smiling goodbye and disappeared over the
side; we were alone and homeward bound, but felt understand-
ably sad as the African coast faded behind us.

Ashanti and the Gold Coast in 1916

*Reprinted by permission of the Hutchinson Publishing Group Ltd.*